"Anyone can bec... ...g person and build a good life if they use the tools from this book."

Respect is a beautiful thing.™

This book is dedicated to my beloved Mom and Dad, who are now both in heaven, for their unconditional love, unwavering positive example, and for teaching me how to be a strong person.

ISBN-13: 978-0-9899152-1-2

Printed and bound in the United States of America.

ATTENTION - SCHOOLS: We provide this book below our cost to teachers who are willing to read it aloud to their students during read-aloud time (it will spark some great discussions) - please see p. 171 for the bulk order form. A free review copy of this book is available upon request to school board members, superintendents, directors of curriculum and instruction, principals, assistant principals, instructional supervisors, school counselors, PTO/PTA presidents, and community leaders by sending an email request to sbookpublishing@gmail.com.)

HOW TO BECOME A STRONG PERSON AND BUILD A GOOD LIFE

JAMES WEGERT, M.ED.
SCHOOL COUNSELOR

Strong Book Publishing
Lancaster, PA

Way too many people think that respect is something that must be received before it's given. They have the "If you respect me, I'll respect you" attitude. In order to create a much better society, may I respectfully suggest that:

- we all need to change our attitude to "I'll give you respect even if you don't give it to me." (The reason for this suggestion is that everyone has already earned the right to respect just by being a person.)

- it's time for everyone - school administrators, school board members, all school staff, parents, students, community leaders, business leaders, and politicians to take positive action to increase the level of respect in our society

- it's time for parents to raise their children to respect their job (which for youth is to be a student), others, and themselves if they're not doing so already

- it's time for schools and the communities that they serve to develop and implement a plan to model, teach, encourage, and recognize respect

Only by uniting and working together will we be able to create a society where everyone is respected - a society that we all can be proud of.

TABLE OF CONTENTS

Everyone is a miracle.™

INTRODUCTION

"Why should I take the time to read this book? I'm busy!"

Many kids are a bit naïve and think that they can change the world. I'm still a kid at heart and this book is my attempt to do just that. I realize that this is probably only a dream that won't happen, but maybe just maybe, the book will spark a wildfire of respect that spreads around the world through those who read it - if it does, wouldn't that be a beautiful thing? (If it doesn't, at least I can say I gave it a shot before I kicked the bucket.)

Unfortunately, the level of respect in our society has dramatically gone downhill over the years. Way too many people don't have the strong respect for their job (which for young people is to be a student), others, and themselves that they need in order to have a good life. This huge problem has many awful symptoms - things like bullying, school and work underachievement, the onset of health problems at an early age, broken families, violence, crime, etc. We have a full-blown "Respect Crisis" on our hands.

To help address this crisis, I decided to write this book and start a unique school club that's designed to help schools, communities, and parents model, teach, encourage, and recognize respect in a fun way (information about Respect Club™ is on p. 169).

I realize that you're busy, but my request is that you slow down just a bit and take the time to read this book from cover to cover (or ask your teacher to read it to your entire class out loud during the school year). I've tried to pack as much useful information as possible into it because as a school counselor I couldn't just sit back and watch students mess up their lives by making bad (disrespectful) choices without trying to do more to help.

As you're reading, at times you may say to yourself, "Who does this guy think he is and how did he come up with all of the stuff in this book?" I'm just a school counselor, who's trying to make a positive difference. I developed the information through making so many bad choices myself, earning 3 college degrees, observing strong people for over 50 years and working with youth for 25 years at the Boys' Club ®, the YMCA ®, a children's home, and in school as a school counselor (no, I'm not 100).

Please forgive me in advance if at times I sound like a know-it-all. The truth is that I don't know-it-all. I'm still learning and trying to practice every day being a strong person.

Unfortunately, this book wasn't written to read like a mystery thriller, keeping you on the edge of your seat as you turn each page. However, it was written for a really exciting purpose - to help readers learn the important tools that are needed to build a good life and then to encourage them to build it! I've mixed in over fifty true stories to make it even more interesting. I think that you'll especially enjoy reading the stories about my bad choices. You probably will be thinking something like, "I can't believe he did that." My hope is that reading about my bad choices and the bad choices of others helps you to avoid making the same ones.

This book uses the word respect as a verb. It defines respect as "showing that someone or something is important by what you say or do." When a person has respect, they take positive action whenever possible. The focus is on others or on something else - not on themselves. So, in other words, this definition means that respect is not something that you are trying to get, but it's something that you are trying to give every day - shockingly, as you'll find out later in the book, even when it's not given to you.

There may be things in this book that you disagree with. In fact, there may be times while reading that you feel like screaming and throwing it against the wall. (For example, you may have felt that way when I mentioned in the last paragraph about giving respect to others who don't give it to you - what?) That's OK. Please just take the things from the book that you agree with and use them to improve your life along with the lives of others.

The book is broken into five parts - Section 1: The basics, Section 2: The five tools of a strong person, Section 3: How to use the five tools to build a good life, Section 4: Other Important "Stuff" and Section 5: More intense stories for ages 15 and up (Caution: these stories are not suitable for students under age 15)

In Section 2, I explain in detail the parts of each tool (for example, the tool of Character has three parts - Honesty, Integrity, and Trustworthiness).

Just like my other books, this book wasn't written to be read once and then forgotten - it was written to be referred back to over and over again - think of it as a roadmap. It can be used by youth, parents, adults - everyone. Isn't it a good idea to have a map before you go on a road (living a good life) that you may have never been on before, that you haven't been on long, that's kind of bumpy, that you're somewhat lost on, or that you're trying to teach your children to go on? Well here goes . . .

True story - miracle: When I tell my students that every person is a miracle, they often say, "I'm not a miracle." Then I say, "OK, let me prove it." I ask them to imagine that every kid in the whole world is standing outside the window of the school as far as the eye can see. Next, I ask them to imagine that there's a huge video screen with their picture on it - so big that everyone can see it and a powerful loudspeaker - so powerful that everyone can hear this announcement: "Anyone who looks exactly like the person on the screen and acts exactly like the person on the screen - please come up front." Then I ask my student, "Would anyone else except you come up front?" They say, "No." I ask, "How could that be? - there are billions and billions of people in the world" - and before they've had a chance to answer I say, "It's because you're a miracle." (I heard on the radio that the odds of 2 people having the same exact DNA is 1 in 406 trillion - I think this proves that each person is indeed a miracle.)

"Unfortunately, we don't seem to see the miracles all around us right in front of our eyes. Think of the sun - a massive ball of hot gases that lights up half of the earth at one time, keeps us warm, makes the plants grow, and never burns up. How does that happen? Think of 50 small birds flying in formation diving, weaving, and changing direction instantly without running into each other. How do they do that? But most of all, think of people - there are about 8 billion people in the world and yet no two people look and act exactly alike (even identical twins). How could this be? . . . it's because they're miracles. Every person deserves to be treated with respect because every person is a miracle."

SECTION 1: THE BASICS

"*The only thing necessary for the triumph of evil is for good people to do nothing.*"
- Edmund Burke

NOTES:

1

WHAT IS A STRONG PERSON?

The first step to becoming a strong person is to know what a strong person is

Based upon my education and over fifty years of life experience interacting with strong people, I've come to the conclusion that a strong person has these five tools:

Character

Attitude

Responsibility

Effort

Self-Control

When you're a strong person, you use these tools every day to respect:

- your **J**ob

- **O**thers

- **Y**ourself

And by doing so, you build a good life.

What is a good life? May I suggest this definition:

1. You are loved, and you give love to others

2. You live at peace with everyone

3. You have completed your education and you have a good job that you enjoy doing - a job that helps to give your life meaning and a sense of purpose

4. You earn enough money in that job to satisfy all of your needs and some of your wants

5. You truly care about other people, and it shows through your words and actions

6. You have some strong friends with whom you have a lot of good clean fun with, who support you through good times and bad, and who hold you accountable for what you say and do

7. You serve other people in some manner

Did you notice what the first letters of the five tools spells? (cares) Did you notice what the first letters of the things that a strong person has respect for spells? (joy)

"Every person is a unique treasure, more valuable than silver or gold - even if they don't have fame, lots of money, a great personality, or good looks. Don't believe anyone who says otherwise."

2

... WHAT'S IN IT FOR ME IF I BECOME A STRONG PERSON?

What am I going to get if I do all of this work to become a strong person?

For people to be really motivated to do something, they first must be convinced that they'll get rewarded in some way if they do it. It's human nature. For example, when I explain to a student what a strong person is and ask them to consider trying to become a strong person, they often say to me, "Why would I do that?" or in other words, "If I put in the daily effort that's required to become a strong person, what's in it for me?"

So here are some of the possible rewards from becoming a strong person:

When you're a strong person, you're more likely to . . .

. . . do your best in school

. . . get financial assistance and scholarship money to pay for your education after high school

. . . get a good job that you enjoy doing in the field of your choice after your education is completed

. . . do excellent work in your first job

. . . be promoted from your first job to a better job, then eventually to an even better job

5

. . . have a real sense of purpose and meaning in your life

. . . feel proud of yourself (even if others don't like you or aren't proud of you for some reason)

. . . not waste your money

. . . be able to afford to live in a good neighborhood

. . . be able to afford to buy a nice car that doesn't break down every few months

. . . be able to find and attract a strong person to date one day - if you choose to do so

. . . have a lifelong loving marriage one day - if you choose to get married

. . . be able to afford to start a family one day - if you choose to do so

. . . be able to afford to take your family on vacation to one of those famous places like the place with the mouse who has big ears (my students get really fired up when I mention this possible reward)

. . . not become addicted to alcohol or other drugs

. . . make and keep strong friends

. . . live at peace with everyone

. . . be able to deal with disrespectful people in a positive way - in other words, be able to not say an unkind (disrespectful) word to anyone regardless of what they say to you

. . . not be too concerned about what disrespectful people say, do, or think (If they don't want to have a good life, that's up to them.)

. . . be able to not let what disrespectful people say and do control you (in other words, you refuse to make yourself angry from what others say or do)

. . . get along with your relatives (or at least respectfully tolerate them)

. . . be able to turn your lemons that come your way into lemonade - in other words, be able to make the best of a bad situation (lemons = problems or things that go wrong in life)

. . . be able to pick yourself up, dust yourself off, apologize, learn, forgive yourself, and move forward after making a bad choice

. . . avoid depression when things aren't going well for you (a strong person asks to see their school counselor and/or gets professional counseling help as needed to improve their mental health)

. . . be healthy in mind, body, and spirit

. . . have lots of good clean fun (including being goofy and silly, having a good laugh, and enjoying the company of others) without needing to be under the influence of alcohol or other drugs

. . . be happy! (in other words - have joy!)

. . . have a good life

I could go on and on - the rewards of being a strong person are almost endless.

A few of my students have told me that they think becoming a strong person "sounds kind of boring and not that fun." Do the possible rewards that I just listed sound boring and not that fun?

Joy story: When we lived in a small town in Virginia, a strong person who was the leader of an organization in our town accepted a new position in Chicago. The organization decided to give him a grand sendoff party - and grand it was. In the banquet room of Ernie's restaurant, one group after another from the organization performed a humorous skit or song honoring the leader. We almost couldn't stop laughing.

The presentation by six senior citizen ladies from the organization was the high point of the evening. The leader rode a big Harley-Davidson® motorcycle for fun, so they dressed up in full length black leather motorcycle outfits and sang on stage the famous old motorcycle song, "The Leader of the Pack." The laughter was almost deafening. At one point during the song, the leader stood on his chair waving his napkin in a big circle above his head with the music blaring to pump up the crowd. I noticed that the restaurant employees standing off to the side were amazed and smiling about what was going on. Everyone was having such a wonderful time. I think we did a great job that night of showing in a small way that living your life as a strong person is exciting and fun. We all had joy.

Now that you've learned the basics and what you can get from becoming a strong person - it's time to explore the five tools of a strong person in more detail. Later in the book I'll explain how the tools can be used to build a good life. Since I love baseball, baseball acronyms are listed below each chapter heading to help you remember the parts of each tool.

As I start the process of teaching my students how to become a strong person, I begin with the My Armor™ lesson. I ask them to imagine that they're a "knight" - which is easy to do because our district-wide school mascot is a "Red Knight." I explain that knights wear armor made of metal for protection from all kinds of things including arrows that fly through the air. I ask them to:

1. Put on their imaginary armor every day before they come to school.

2. Remember that they're a good person no matter what disrespectful people say or do.

3. Be ready for imaginary arrows (disrespectful things that people say or do) that are going to come their way.

4. Have the plan of letting those arrows just bounce off of their armor (sometimes even by acting like they didn't hear what a disrespectful student said to them)*

5. Not be a person who shoots arrows at others (for any reason)

6. Immediately switch to using "My Shield"™ if they start to feel angry or have any other strong emotion (My Shield is explained on pp. 40-43)

9

Unfortunately, way too many of us are in the habit of shooting arrows at others (saying or doing disrespectful things - especially after someone has shot an arrow at us). Please keep in mind that shooting arrows isn't right, and it doesn't help you or the other person to have a good life. If it's not kind, please choose to be strong and just don't say or do it!

I emphasize to my students repeatedly that **the most important part of "My Armor" is number 5.** The reason I do this is because I've seen so many students mess up their lives by being a person who shoots arrows.

*I tell my students that my goal before they get to fifth grade is to help them to get their armor so thick and strong that any verbal arrow will just bounce right off and fall harmlessly to the ground.

"Right is right, even if everyone is against it, and wrong is wrong, even if everyone is for it."
- William Penn

NOTES:

SECTION 2: THE FIVE TOOLS OF A STRONG PERSON – CHARACTER, ATTITUDE, RESPONSIBILITY, EFFORT, AND SELF-CONTROL

(In Chapter 3 through Chapter 7, when you see a dot indented like the one below, it means that one part of the tool that you're learning about is going to be described.

-

For example, the tool of Character has three parts: honesty, integrity, and trustworthiness.)

Have you ever noticed how hard it is to get almost everyone to agree on something? Interestingly, everyone who I talked with during the two-year process of writing, rewriting, and editing this book wholeheartedly agreed that the low level of respect in our society is a huge problem and that we need to find a positive way to increase it in order to make the world a better place.

"If you really want to change the world, start with the children."

"Children are the world's most valuable resource and its best hope for the future."
- President Kennedy

The Respect Club Motto: *Respect Always!*™

3

CHARACTER

(Baseball acronym for the parts of this tool = HIT)

- <u>h</u>onesty - a strong person doesn't lie, deceive, cheat or steal

Unfortunately, many people choose to lie when they're very young to stay out of trouble. I did. My parents helped me learn not to lie by giving me twice the punishment whenever I tried to lie my way out of something. So, if I broke something while fooling around and then tried to lie my way out of it by saying it was an "accident" and my parents found out the truth, I would get twice as much punishment.

Honesty story #1: It's very sad and shocking to me how many students have learned to lie at a young age to try to avoid punishment for a bad choice.

Way back when I was a substitute teacher for a first-grade class, I had a break because I didn't have recess supervision duty that day. After recess ended, the first student who walked in from outside told me, "Sally is out on the playground crying because Billy pushed her down."

When Billy came in, I asked him, "I heard that Sally is out on the playground crying." He immediately said, "She is?" I then asked him, "Billy, what did you do?" He said, "I didn't do anything." I asked again. This time he said, "She tripped over her own two feet and fell down." I asked again. He said, "The other kids told me to do it." I asked again and he finally said, "I pushed her down." It took me asking the same question four times to get to the truth.

Honesty story #2: One day while driving to work, I saw a nice heavy duty shiny wrench, the kind that people use to work on cars, laying about 10 feet into the road. I had several choices at that point: a. Steal it. b. Forget about it, because it wasn't my wrench and it wasn't my problem if someone ran it over and broke it. c. Run it over on purpose to break it. d. Go door to door and ask people if they know who the wrench belongs to e. Something else. Since I had to get to work, I asked myself the question, "What would you want someone else to do if that was your wrench?" I decided to move the wrench out of the street and put it on the curb so that hopefully the person who lost it would find it and so that no one would run it over.

Honest story #3: When I was in 2nd grade, kids in the neighborhood loved racing small plastic toy race cars that were powered by windup rubber bands. You turned a knob on the back of the car, that twisted a rubber band located underneath the car, and the power of the untwisting of the rubber band turned the wheels. My brother's car was red, our next-door neighbor's car was blue (and the fastest), and the boy who lived two doors down from us had a green car. I think that my brother designed a track that the cars raced on. It had wooden rails on the sides to keep the cars heading in the same direction.

I didn't have the money needed to buy myself a car to race, so if I remember correctly, my brother and I came up with a bad idea of how I could "win" one. Somehow, we got everyone who lived near us to agree to pay a small entry fee to be in a big race and that the money would be used to buy the winner a new car. We rigged the race by asking our next-door neighbor if I could use his blue car for the race (he was not going to be home on the day of the race), almost making it a sure thing that I would win. Using the neighbor's car, I "won" the race, and my prize was an orange car. This was a bad choice. It was not honest. I should have just waited and saved up the money to buy a car of my own.

14

Honesty story #4: Sadly, I chose to cheat in Mrs. Wetzel's 3rd grade class by copying the words, "wages" and "avenue" off of the spelling test paper of the smartest kid in the class so that I would get an "A". I regretted making this choice and I felt bad about it. I got a grade that I didn't earn. This bad feeling helped me to never cheat again.

Honesty story #5: Senior year of high school was almost over. Pretty much all we had left to do was take our final exams - and then we would work at a summer job and go off to college in the fall.

Our chemistry teacher asked if we could be trusted to take the exam unsupervised in a small library on the second floor of Mayfield High School while she taught a lesson to the rest of the class. We all said, "Yes!"

The teacher left and things went well for about 35 minutes until Wendy said something like, "Oh, (bad word), just give me your paper Jim!", as she snatched my paper away from me and immediately started to copy answers from it.

I said, "Hey, give me that back!", but she didn't listen. I told her that we were going to get into trouble if she didn't give it back. She ignored me until out of the corner of her eye she saw the teacher coming up the hall - and then she tried to throw my test paper to me. I can still picture the paper floating through the air and me trying and failing to catch it before it hit the floor.

It turned out the teacher had seen her throw it and she was not happy. She immediately went up to Wendy and said, "Wendy, were you cheating?" Sadly, Wendy looked the teacher right in the eye and said "No!" Sadly, she refused to be honest and take responsibility for her actions - even as a senior in high school.

15

Honesty story #6. When I was a middle school counselor, a student (I'm sorry that I don't remember his name, so let's just call him Jeff) came to my office and said that he was upset because he got an afterschool detention from his social studies teacher, Mr. Berger, for "no reason." I asked him if he had a friend in the class who could back up his story. He said "yes" so I called his friend down to my office. I asked his friend what Jeff had done in class to get a detention. He quickly answered, "Well he did this . . ., then he did this . . ., and finally he did this."

While his friend was telling me the truth, Jeff's mouth was wide open in astonishment. His friend saw this, looked at him, and said, "You didn't expect me to lie for you - did you?" This student's honesty was one of the highlights of my job as a middle school counselor.

Throughout your life you're going to have many opportunities to lie, deceive, cheat, steal or otherwise be dishonest. I encourage you to rise up, be strong, and make the good choice not to do any of these things. It can lead to all kinds of problems and doing these things isn't right. If you've done these things in the past - now is a great time to admit what you've done, apologize if possible, make up for it if you can, learn from your bad choices, forgive yourself, and go back to trying to be strong.

- **i**ntegrity - a strong person does what they say they're going to do. In other words, they're a person of their word. If they say that they're going to do something, they do it - even if they don't feel like doing it. (Of course, this does not apply to situations where you make the bad choice of saying that you're going to do something that you know is a bad choice.)

Integrity story #1: You may have never seen a ravine - but it's a steep-sided valley that usually has a creek running through it at the bottom. I used to live across the street from one which was about 100 yards wide (like a football field), 150 feet deep (like fifteen basketball goals stacked on top of each other), and over a mile long.

Back then people didn't have the fancy mulching lawn mowers that grind up grass clippings like many people have now. Instead, the mowers had a grass catcher on the back of them to collect the cut grass as it came out of the mower. Most people stuffed their clippings into trash bags and then put the bags out weekly with their trash.

So that we wouldn't have to waste time bagging our clippings, our close friends of many years who lived on the other side of the street, gave us permission to dump them over the edge of the ravine just to the left of their garage. Of course, they only gave us permission to dump clippings, not trash.

One day while I was dumping a large box filled with clippings, I somehow lost control of it and over the edge it went. The box fell about 20 feet down before it got stuck on the weeds that were sticking out from the side of the ravine. Unlike some other areas of the ravine where you could walk down a steep path to the bottom, the place where I dropped the box was a dangerous cliff.

I walked back home and told my dad what happened. He said, "Let's go, we have to be a good neighbor and not leave trash in the middle of the cliff." So, to make a long story short - after a failed attempt to lower me down the cliff with me hanging onto the end of a long pole with one hand and trying to grab the box with the other, he decided to tie a garden hose around my waist and lower me down to where the box was. I was afraid that I was going to fall, but my dad assured me that I was going to be all right. I was able to grab the box and he pulled me back up. That day my dad taught me that it's very important to have integrity - to do what you say that you're going to do. I also learned the importance of respect for the property of others.

Integrity story #2: After seven years working as a Director at a YMCA and being laid off - and then working for another seven years as a Director at Community Center (similar to a YMCA) and resigning because the Community Center building was sold (if you are age 15 and up, please read the full story on p. 153-154) - I was faced with having to make a mid-life career change.

My wife didn't want to move from Lancaster because it's a nice city, we know people here, and her parents live here. I carefully investigated several possible careers including becoming a school counselor. I talked with school counselors in our area as well as with teachers who worked with me during the summer at YMCA Camp Shand (which was the 3rd oldest YMCA sleepaway camp in the United States). Everyone I talked with thought that I would make a good school counselor.

I talked with my sweet wife about the possibility of going back to school to get another master's degree to become qualified as a school counselor. Her first question was, "How much is that going to cost?" I told her that we were going to have to take out a $40,000 loan and I was going to have to work part-time selling appliances while going to school full-time to help pay the bills.
I think that she was rightfully nervous about going into that much debt, but she was willing to let me give it a try. I told her that I would give it my best to become a school counselor. She trusted me.

I started graduate school with the mindset that since I was at least fifteen years older than the other students, I was going to have to get all A's in order to be able to get a job after graduation.

Although it wasn't easy and I had to stay up until 4 a.m. on some nights writing papers for my classes, I was able to have integrity and keep my word to her.

Integrity story #3: I also would like to mention that during our wedding ceremony my wife promised me that she would love me all the way until death. She has shown integrity by keeping her word for over thirty years!

- trustworthiness - a strong person can be trusted in all situations. More and more employers are saying that they're having a problem finding employees who can be trusted to not steal from them. Also, millions and millions of friendships/relationships each year are damaged or broken because one or both people have been untrustworthy. Please choose to save heartache for everyone by being a trustworthy person.

Trustworthiness story #1: When I was a freshman in college, my dad suggested that I take NROTC classes that would qualify me to be an officer in the United States Navy when I graduated from college.

During the winter in Ohio, about forty other people who were taking these classes were invited to fly down on a military cargo plane to sunny warm Pensacola, Florida to spend a few days visiting the Naval Air Station where Navy pilots were trained.

During part of the visit, we were taken to an indoor pool where pilots were trained in how to safely escape from their plane if it crashed into the ocean. At one end of the pool was a large contraption called the "Dilbert Dunker" that kind of looked like the first hill of a roller coaster. But it was different. Instead of going up the hill, a single roller coaster car with a metal cage around it, to simulate the cockpit of a plane, started at the top of the hill and then rapidly came down and crashed into the water. The track of the roller coaster extended out into the water and then after entering the water the track turned sharply in the opposite direction making the roller coaster car go quickly upside down.

19

The "Dilbert Dunker" is designed to simulate what happens when a plane crashes into the water. Unfortunately, some Navy pilots have died unnecessarily because they became disoriented after a crash. Instead of swimming toward the surface, they sadly swam toward the bottom.

The drill sergeant asked the group if anyone was willing to volunteer to try out the "Dilbert Dunker." For some reason, without really thinking, I raised my hand to volunteer. The drill sergeant gave me instructions and I tried to listen carefully.

To give me the full experience, they had me put on a parachute which was like carrying a backpack with a fifty pound weight in it. I walked up the metal stairs, sat down in the "cockpit" (the single roller coaster car), and they strapped me in.

The good thing about the straps was that they were all attached to one buckle, which meant that I could release the straps quickly by just moving the latch on the buckle.

At the bottom of each side of the track that went into the pool I noticed two frogmen (people with scuba gear on) looking up at me. I was just about to find out for myself what it's like when your plane crashes into the ocean. Later, several people from my group told me that they could see fear in my face - fear like I thought that I was going to die.

Suddenly a bell rang, and I found myself hurling toward the water. Then the "plane" crashed into the water, and I was instantly flipped upside down. I quickly hit the latch, the straps were released, and I started swimming out of the "cockpit" while the two frogmen looked at me intently to be sure that I was OK and that they didn't have to rescue me.

When I got up to the surface, I was feeling proud of myself. That feeling didn't last long. I swam over to the large raft that was in the pool and started to pull myself into it. All of a sudden, the drill sergeant running toward me and screaming, "What are your doing!!", "Didn't you listen!" and "If you get into the raft with your parachute on, the sharp parts of the parachute mechanism will pop it!"

I was embarrassed because I hadn't listened well enough to remember this part of his instructions. I took off my parachute and got into the raft without any more problems.

I trusted everyone that day, especially the frogmen who would have saved me from drowning if needed.

Trustworthiness story #2*: Speaking of saving someone from drowning, that's what my brother Tom almost did when he was five years old. When I was one year old, my mom, dad, brother, and I traveled to Old Man's Cave in Ohio. The park is famous for several natural wonders including waterfalls and whirlpools (to see a whirlpool, please search online for "video of whirlpool at Old Man's Cave")

The park has wooden boardwalks throughout it to keep visitors away from areas that are dangerous. Soon after we arrived, we decided to split up with my mom and me going in one direction and my dad and brother going in the other.

As he walked along with my brother, something in the distance caught my dad's attention and he decided to go off the boardwalk with my brother to get a better look. As he got closer to something that looked like a small pool of water, he crouched down and suddenly, he slipped and fell in.

The problem was that the water was up to his neck, and he couldn't get out because the sides were slippery - which meant that there was nothing for him to grab onto to pull himself out.

21

Thankfully my brother didn't fall in also. My dad trusted my brother and told him something like, "Go back to the boardwalk where we were walking and tell some people that my dad fell into a hole and needs help to get out."

My brother did as he was told, and quickly he was able to find a few men who were willing to go with him to rescue my dad. Before he led them to the place where my dad had fallen in, my dad appeared soaking wet from head to toe. He had found a way to pull himself out. He thanked the men for their willingness to help.

That day my dad learned that it's important, even for adults - to follow the rules. He also learned that my brother could be trusted - even at five years old and in an emergency.

*My brother provided the details of this story because I was too young to remember.

Trustworthiness story #3: My first job was working at Kenny King's restaurant near Cleveland, Ohio. Back then, Kenny King's was one of the few restaurants in the United States that could be its own restaurant and have Kentucky Fried Chicken® as part of their menu.

I started out as a busboy/dishwasher and eventually got promoted to working in the take-out shop where people came to pick up their chicken. We were busy - lots of chicken flew out of there.

One day my boss asked me if I wanted to drive a large catering order for a church youth group event on the other side of Cleveland. I loaded two very large aluminum tins of chicken to the trunk of my parents' car (probably over 300 pieces of chicken) and off I went.

If you can believe it, back then there was no such thing as a GPS and I had to follow the directions that my boss had written out. I was having difficulty finding the place and I was starting to get a bit panicky because it looked like I was going to be late.

To my right, I saw a long row of tall bushes and looking in-between the bushes I thought I saw . . . a church! I turned down a side street and into a parking lot. Just then I saw a few people walking up the church steps. I quickly jumped out of the car and yelled, "Is this the _____ (I don't remember the name) church?

Back then you could lift up the outside door handle of a Toyota to lock the car door without a key. Since I had locked the door so many times like this in the past, I did it without thinking as I yelled out.

Then a horrible feeling came over me. I realized that I had just locked the car door with the keys inside, with the motor running, and with the hot chicken locked in the trunk.

This was a pretty big lemon (problem) at the time (lemons in life are explained in detail on pp. 121-132).

Just like most human minds often do, especially when something goes wrong, my mind went right to the negative. I thought, "I'm going to get fired for this."

I went into the church and told the husband-and-wife youth group leaders about my problem. The husband wasn't very empathetic and quickly said, "Well, we'll just get the chicken from somewhere else!"

Thankfully his wife had empathy for me, and she tried to find a way to solve the problem in a positive way. She asked, "Is there someone else who has the key to the car?" I said, "Yes, but the spare key is at my parents' house across town."

She asked her husband if he would drive me home to get the key. He reluctantly said he would, and we sped off. He drove almost like a NASCAR® driver with lots of acceleration and braking - and we were able to make it back with the key in about 45 minutes.

When we entered the church parking lot, we saw about six youth group members standing by the door of my parents' car. They had straightened out a coat hanger and bent it into a hook at the end. Then they decided to shove it through the rubber molding between the doors (tearing up the molding and doing about $50 in damage).

As we walked up to them, we saw that they had succeeded in hooking the key and they were in the process of pulling it out of the ignition.

I asked them to stop because I now had the key (and I didn't want them to do any more damage). I thanked them for trying to get the key out (even though I knew my parents would not be happy about the damage).

Thankfully the chicken was still hot when we opened the tins from the trunk.

When I finally got back to Kenny King's, my manager just laughed and laughed. He trusted me to get the job done and I delivered (pun intended).

Reflection: Do you think that the tool of "Character" can help you to build a good life? If so, why? If not, why not?

4

ATTITUDE

(Baseball acronym for the parts of this tool = CCFFHREB)

- **c**aring - a strong person truly cares about other people; they treat others in a caring manner; they're interested in how others are doing; they're patient and kind with others, they're not all wrapped up in themselves and their own problems; they have manners - they do things like holding doors and letting others go first, they say things like "please", "thank you", and "I'm sorry."

Caring story: Back on p. 19, I mentioned my NROTC trip to Florida. One day during that trip we were given some time off, so my friend and I decided to rent a small sailboat from a rental place located right on a small bay. The problem was that we didn't know how to sail at all.

Things started out well, but soon the wind caught our sail, and we flipped over (of course we had our lifejackets on) and fell into pretty cold water. We were able to turn the sailboat right-side up by pulling on the wooden rudder which stuck out from the bottom of the boat. The same thing happened again.

We mistakenly thought that we were getting the hang of sailing when we flipped again. This time we had a real problem because the rudder had come loose and was floating away from us. We now had no way to turn the sailboat back over.

We didn't panic while we were hanging on to the upside-down sailboat. Instead, we both waved our hands and yelled "help" toward the place where we had rented the boat. Thankfully, the owner saw us, and soon he drove his motorboat out to help us.

When we got the sailboat upright again, I asked my friend if he wanted to keep sailing. He was cold and said, "No, let's sail back to the rental place and go home, I've had enough."

As we sailed back, the rental place was to the right and a yacht club with fancy sailboats and yachts (big motorboats) was on the left. We started drifting toward the yacht club even though we were trying to get to the rental place.

We kept going more and more left and we didn't know how to go right. Now our sailboat was completely up against the end of the long dock of the yacht club. A lady came running down the dock and asked us if we needed help. I said "Yes", and she offered me her hand so that I could hold on and step off the sailboat on to the dock.

Much to our surprise, at that moment the wind caught the sail and started to move the boat away from the dock. Unfortunately, I couldn't let go of her hand quickly enough and I accidentally pulled her into the water, the sailboat flipped over again, and now all three of us were in the water. When we surfaced, she cheerfully said, "Hi, my name is Linda."

Just then her husband came running down the dock and yelled, "Honey, what are you doing? - We have a dinner reservation in ten minutes!!" He was not happy.

She explained what happened and her husband calmed himself down. He offered to help us sail the boat back to the rental place and we gladly accepted his offer.

In this story the owner of the rental place cared for us when we lost our rudder (possibly just because he wanted his sailboat back in one piece), Linda cared for us when she offered her hand to help us at the dock and her husband cared for us by helping us to get the sailboat safely back to the rental place. (We were very thankful to be back on dry ground.)

It may be hard to believe in today's me, me, me world, but people who really care about others (selflessness) are happier in the long run than people who are all about themselves (selfishness). If you don't think this is true, please check out the research online (more information about the danger of selfishness can be found on pp. 133-136.).

> cheerful - Unfortunately, many people have an uncheerful (negative) attitude - and they have some type of excuse for why they have this type of attitude – usually because they've had or have lemons (problems) in their life. These people can seem to find the negative in almost anything. These people like to complain. They don't understand that having this type of attitude doesn't help them or anyone else around them - it's just become a habit.

> Instead, a strong person tries to be as cheerful as possible in all situations, they try to brighten the day of others and maybe even try to make them laugh. They do their best to put a smile on their face, even when they don't feel like it. They realize that it's not easy to be positive when things are going wrong, when they don't get their way, when they get accused of doing something they didn't do, when someone tells a lie about them, or when they're feeling frustrated/angry, etc. - but they still try to do it every day. In other words, they try their best to find something positive in almost everything.

> A person with a cheerful attitude is not a complainer. (Please see p. 107 for a story about complaining.)

Cheerful story: In my job as a school counselor, I really try to be one of the most positive and cheerful people in the school.

After all, what student wants to talk to a school counselor who's grumpy? The truth is that sometimes I don't really feel cheerful, but I try to fake it anyway. Interestingly, as I'm faking it, I often start to feel more cheerful (especially after I get a wave or a smile from a student or if I get a laugh from a staff person when I tell them a silly joke.) As you'll see on pp. 122-125, my dad did a great job of faking being cheerful even when he really wasn't feeling that way.

I must confess, and my wife can confirm, that I need to work on being more cheerful at home when something goes wrong or someone else in the family has an uncheerful (negative) attitude. (All of us are still a work in progress - no one has it all together.)

- **f**riendly - A strong person is willing to be a strong friend to others, including being willing to be a strong friend to someone who's ignored or rejected by others

You may be asking yourself, "Why is being friendly and having strong friends so important?" The reason is that we're not meant to go through life alone. My suggestion is that you find a group of strong friends to be a part of in your neighborhood, in school, in a school club, on a team, at your place of work, in an community organization, etc. Please be part of a group of friends who are interested in making good choices and having a good life. Sometimes it's hard to find this group and it often takes time to do so - but it's well worth the effort. (When I talk about being friendly, I realize that you don't have the time to be everyone's strong friend - but please try to be polite and kind to everyone.)

Strong friends will talk with you, encourage you, and help you through the downs of life. They'll celebrate with you during the ups of life, help you to stay focused on making good choices every day, help you resist negative peer pressure, give you good advice when needed and hold you accountable for your actions. Hopefully, they'll be a strong friend for your entire life.

A strong friend:

- allows you to be yourself, really listens to you, and doesn't share what's been said (they do share if you mention something about hurting yourself - in that case they immediately tell a respected adult, like your teacher or school counselor, so that you can get help - and they continue asking for help until you get it.)

- can be trusted, supports you, helps you, treats you with respect, and sticks with you even when things aren't going well for you and/or when you make bad choices

- never encourages you to make a bad (disrespectful) choice

- encourages you to make a good (respectful) choice - even when disrespectful people are encouraging you to make a bad choice

- tells you what you need to hear even when you don't want to hear it

- does things like grab your upper arm, when necessary, in order to pull you away from a bad situation while saying something like, "Oh no, let's go, there's not going to be a fight. It's not worth it."

- is willing to forgive you when you mess up

- comes and talks with you as soon as possible when there's a problem in the friendship

- understands that friendships change and can accept those changes after talking it out

Friendly story #1: When I encourage my elementary school students to be friendly, they sometimes mistakenly think that I'm asking them to try to be a strong friend to everyone. I explain to them that even though they don't have enough time to do this, they can still try their best to be kind to everyone.

Friendly story #2: I had a tough time finding a group of strong friends because I started school when I was four years old and up until 8th grade, I was the youngest and shortest kid - and this made me an easy target for bullies. Many people did not want to be my friend because I wasn't cool. The good news is that I eventually made a few strong friends after I learned how to be a strong friend. I also learned how to look for people who needed a strong friend and who were willing to be a strong friend to me.

I went to a new school for 12th grade and to begin with I didn't have any friends. I can still remember going into the cafeteria for the first time and feeling all alone. I looked around and I saw a guy who was sitting all alone away from all the other tables. I decided to take a risk, walked over, and asked him, "Is it OK if I sit here?" He said, "Sure, go ahead." I made a friend that day.

Just a word of warning about spending too much time with people who regularly make bad (disrespectful) choices regularly - you tend to become more like the people you hang with, so if you spend a lot of time with disrespectful people, it's more likely that you'll also make bad choices and partially mess up your life. Unfortunately, as a school counselor I've seen this happen way too many times - a good kid with good grades starts to hang with people who regularly make bad choices and soon their school achievement and behavior goes downhill dramatically.

- **f**orgiving - A strong person is willing to forgive others who treat them with disrespect - even if the other person isn't sorry for what they've done

Forgiving story #1: When I ask my students to consider forgiving someone who's treated them with disrespect, many times they bluntly say, "I'm not doing that!" This is especially the case when the person who treated them poorly isn't sorry for what they've done - and I can understand that. When I make this request, I usually also ask the student if they think that I'm trying to help the other person involved or if I'm trying to help them. They usually say that I'm trying to help the other person. I say something like, "No, I'm trying to help you because if you refuse to forgive other people it doesn't help you because you're more likely to become an angry person - and an angry person is less likely to have a good life."

Forgiving story #2: One day when I was a middle school counselor, a seventh grader told me that he gets really angry every time that he sees another student because the other student had "embarrassed" him back in fourth grade. I paused for a moment and then said something like, "Fourth grade? - that was three years ago, do you think that all fourth graders really know what they're doing? . . . don't you think that it's time to just let it go?" He thought about it a bit and then thankfully he agreed that it was time to forgive and move forward.

Forgiving story #3: The truth is that I had some problems during childhood forgiving others - even when someone did something that really wasn't a big deal.

As a kid I lived in a house on the corner that had pretty big backyard. It also had a concrete patio that doubled as a basketball court. The yard was surrounded by hedges (large bushes) that were about 6 feet high. We had great times playing all kinds of games there including wiffle ball (a homerun was if you hit it over the hedge in center field), basketball, touch football, and even a tackle football game against the Fremont Whips* in full football gear (to get someone out of bounds we pushed them into the hedges, we even had cheerleaders and a

31

real scoreboard with changeable numbers made from cardboard).

We usually had to go door-to-door trying to round up enough kids for a game. Often when we went to Steve's house, who lived right across the street, to ask his mother if he could come out and play, she would grumpily say "No!" The guys and I got tired of her almost always saying "no" and her negative attitude.

One day a few guys and I were shooting baskets on the patio, and I noticed that Steve's mother was about to leave in her car. I heard her yell out something like, "I'm going to the store (located about a mile away), I'll be back soon."

Since I hadn't forgiven her for being grumpy, almost instantly I came up with a bad idea in order to get back at her (revenge is never a good choice regardless of how wronged you feel - it only makes things worse - sometimes it even leads to a continuous cycle of revenge that eventually destroys lives.)

I said to the guys, "She'll be back soon, so why don't we all pick up crabapples (crabapples are small apples that are about the size of a marble) from the ground underneath our crabapple tree, fill both of our hands, hide behind the hedges, wait until she comes back, and then throw as many crabapples as we can over hedges and onto her car."

The guys enthusiastically went along with my bad idea. We all quickly picked up crabapples and got into position kneeling behind the hedges. I watched for her return, and it didn't take long. As soon as I saw her big maroon Chevy turn the corner, I yelled "Now!" and probably close to a hundred crabapples went up over the hedge and bounced off of her car with small thuds in rapid-fire fashion. She slammed on her brakes, jumped out of the car, left her car door open and the motor running, and ran to the back gate of our yard yelling.

All the other guys immediately ran out of our yard through a cut in the hedges that led to the neighbor's backyard. For some reason, I stayed on the patio for a few seconds. She saw me and yelled at me. I then ran away the same way the other guys did. I knew that I'd messed up and I was panicky. I wondered where the guys had gone so that I could meet up with them. I figured that they'd gone to Joey's house on the next street over because they ran in that direction.

When I got to Joey's house, there was no sign of them. I called out Joey's name a couple of times and then finally I heard a quiet voice coming from inside Joey's garage saying, "We're in here." As I walked into the garage, I found the guys hiding there covering their heads with cardboard boxes. Everyone knew that they were in trouble.

Soon I heard my mother yelling my name. (Whenever my mom yelled or my dad whistled while I was playing in the yard or down the street, I was taught to yell "coming" and to come home.)

When I got home in a few minutes, her car was still in the middle of the street with broken pieces of crabapples all over the hood and windshield. She was angry and she was telling my mom something like, "You've got to do something with your son, he needs to be punished." My mom was calm even though Steve's mother was raising her voice and was telling her what to do. My mom told her that she would take care of it, and she sent me in the house.

Thankfully my mother had mercy on me when she came inside. She told me something like, "Don't do anything like that again." I was surprised that I didn't get a big punishment.

I learned a lot from making one bad choice after the other. I learned that it was wrong for not forgiving Steve's mother for her grumpiness, wrong to think up a plan to get revenge on her, wrong for asking others to make bad choices by participating in the plan, wrong for signaling them when to attack, wrong for throwing crabapples, and wrong trying to avoid taking responsibility by running away. Thankfully, Steve's mother didn't lose control of her car and have a wreck.

*By the way, Fremont was the name of the street next to ours. The motto of their football team was "We're going to whip you!" They did, something like 35-7.

Forgiving story #4: One summer afternoon during an intense competitive wiffle ball game in the backyard I got into a heated argument with a guy from down the street. I think his name was Tim. The argument was about whether or not he was "out" at home plate. I insisted that he was out, and he insisted that he was safe. He lost his temper and punched me in the face. I punched him back and then the fight continued with him and I exchanging punches one at a time trying to hit each other harder with each punch.

Finally, after a punch from Tim, I lost it completely. I screamed at the top of my lungs for him to get out of our yard and to never ever come back. I was really mad, possibly the angriest that I've ever been.

Unfortunately, I didn't just "let it go." I refused to forgive him. In fact, I held on to this grudge probably close to a year. Every couple of weeks or so he would show up at the gate of our yard asking to play in whatever game that was going on. I remember looking at him and then being really rude by sharply saying, "No, go!" while pointing in the direction of his house down the street. He never apologized, but finally I let things go and let him come back and play in the yard again. Bottom line, holding on to my anger and refusing to forgive Tim didn't do him or me any good. It was wrong.

- **h**elpful - a strong person tries to help others as much as possible when they have the opportunity because it's a good (respectful) choice - and because they realize that everyone needs help at times and someday it's more than likely that they'll need help from someone. A strong person sees a need during their everyday life and tries to meet that need when it's safe to do so. They even help others in an emergency when it's not safe to do so - like pulling an injured person out of a burning car that is about to explode.

Helpful story #1: A young lady once asked a few other guys and me to help her move her stuff to another apartment. We all thought that she just needed us to load and unload the rented moving van. When we got there, we were shocked to find out that she hadn't even started packing. When we rolled our eyes in frustration as we looked at all of the stuff that wasn't packed, she said, "Sorry, I didn't have time to get everything packed up!" What was supposed to be a two-hour job turned into at least a four-hour job. The good news is that we didn't give up and say, "Call us when you've got everything packed up." Instead, we helped her pack and then we helped her move. We turned a bad situation into something good - an adventure. I even got to drive the big moving truck with the huge steering wheel that was hard to turn because no one else wanted to!

Helpful story #2: While my dad and I were out running errands when I was about ten, he asked me what job I might like in the future. I told him that one day I wanted to get a job that helps people. He smiled and said something like, "That's a nice idea, but you also have to be sure to do something that pays the bills."

Since I didn't know what I wanted to do for a job by the time I was a senior in high school, my dad suggested that I go to college and study business administration so that I could get a job that "pays the bills." I followed his advice, graduated from college, and then worked as a Food Service Manager at Miami University in Ohio for a few years.

I liked the job, but I didn't feel like I was really helping anyone very much, so I decided to go to graduate school to become qualified as a Boys' Club® or a YMCA® Director. Years later, I decided to go back to graduate school again to become qualified as a school counselor.

So, for almost twenty-five years I've tried to be helpful to young people by teaching them the skills that they need to respect their job, others, and themselves.

Helpful story #3: If you can believe it, even though our school is 55 years old, it did not have an elevator in it until last year - even though it has three floors. I can still picture in my mind students with an injured leg or foot hopping on their good foot while holding onto the railing in order to make it up or down the stairs. Right beside them was a helpful student volunteer who was carrying things like their books and backpack while trying to make sure that the injured student didn't fall. Over the years I have seen many students being helpful in all kinds of situations. Being helpful to others is a great thing.

- **r**espectful - a strong person treats other people with respect, as someone who's important - even people who don't treat them with respect and/or people who they don't like. May I suggest that every person who is disrespectful to others is really saying "I need help." They need help because they don't understand that being disrespectful isn't right and it doesn't help anyone. When you're respectful, you don't say or do anything disrespectful for any reason.

36

Respectful story - #1: Unfortunately, this is a story of when I made the bad choice of coming up with a really disrespectful idea for no reason and convincing others to go along with my bad idea.

My parents saved up for many years to have enough money to take us to Florida for a vacation during winter break. We stayed at the Pink Shell© cottages which were small pink cottages that slept four people that were up on 10-foot-high stilts to protect them in case a hurricane hit the area (which it unfortunately did in 2022). The cottages were located right near the beach.

We went on the trip with another family with whom we had been friends for years - the Shultz's. Their family also had two children - Rick, a well-built junior in high school and Susie who was a sophomore in high school. Rick and my brother Tom were on different high school basketball teams.

We had a great time together, including being able to swim outside in nice warm weather. I remember thinking something like, "Wow, this is the life."

A younger boy was staying in a cottage next to us and for some reason he spent hours and hours each day digging a bigger and bigger hole in the sand (maybe because he didn't have anyone to play with). First thing every morning he seemed to really enjoy jumping into that hole.

One night all four children decided to take a walk along the beach. As we were walking, we came upon a dead stingray that had washed up on the beach.

I quickly came up with a really bad idea. I said, "Why don't we find a way to get the stingray back to our cottage and then put it in that big hole so that the boy would have a real surprise when he jumped in. What a cruel idea - what was I thinking??

37

I thought for a second and then said, "As we walked down the beach, I think that we passed some old plywood - why don't we slide it under the stingray and use it to carry it back to the cottage."

Everyone went along with my bad idea. Together we found the wood, pushed it underneath the stingray, lifted it up, and then started to carry it back. The stingray was heavier than we thought it would be and it was slow going as we walked through the sand. Someone suggested that we take a shortcut to the nearby road where it would be easier to walk.

When we were about halfway back things started to fall apart - literally. We heard a small cracking noise coming from the plywood - but for some reason we ignored it and just kept walking.

Suddenly, the plywood broke in half, the tail of the stingray swung around, and the stinger of the stingray hit Rick in the leg drawing blood.

Unfortunately, Rick lost it and started yelling, "I'm going to die!" He was hysterical (out of control). We tried to calm him down by encouraging him to take deep breaths and by telling him that everything was going to be alright, but it didn't work.

He said, "I don't want to walk because that will spread the venom." The three of us had to carry Rick all the way back to the cottage. We couldn't call anyone for help on a cell phone because they didn't exist back then.

As we were carrying him back, I remember looking way back down the road to see a car with its headlights on swerving around the stingray and the plywood that we had just left in the middle of the road.

The parents helped us to get Rick into the cottage. My mother asked him if he wanted some food before he went to the hospital. He said, "No, I don't want it to be my last meal."

Thankfully it turned out that all Rick needed was a tetanus shot to prevent an infection - no venom had gone into his leg.

All of this wouldn't have happened if I had been respectful to the boy in the cottage next to ours. Instead, I made the bad choice of planning to do something disrespectful to someone who had done nothing to me. I tried to learn from this bad choice and move forward.

Respectful story #2: When I suggest to students that they consider treating everyone with respect including those who treat them with disrespect, they often say, "I'm not doing that!" I ask them why and they say, "They don't deserve my respect and also being respectful to them makes me look like a wimp." I tell them that I understand how they feel, but then I ask, "Is disrespecting people who disrespect you helping you or helping them?" Some answer that being disrespectful after being disrespected helps them because they feel like they've stood up for themselves and that sometimes the other person stops running their mouth after being verbally blasted. Others admit that being disrespectful back to others often makes the situation worse and sometimes leads to violence.

Let's step back and look at the key question hidden behind all of this, "Is being disrespectful ever a good choice?" For something to be a good choice it has to have a good purpose, it has to help all of the people involved, it has to help make things better, it has to move you closer to your long-term goals, and it has to be right.

Even though being disrespectful back may be what you feel like doing, I hope that you can see that it doesn't have any of the qualities of a good choice. When you make the bad choice to be disrespectful, you're teaching the other person through your actions that it's OK to be disrespectful - because you're doing it. Do you really want to teach someone something that doesn't help them to have a good life and that could possibly even cause them to get badly hurt or worse someday?

You may be asking yourself, "OK, so what do you suggest I do when someone says something disrespectful to me and I'm feeling angry?" I suggest that you use "My Shield™." Using it has helped my students and me to keep anger and other strong emotions under control.

"My Shield" consists of five parts:

1. STOP - this means that you stop (you don't do anything) instead of just saying or doing something disrespectful right back after someone says or does something disrespectful to you.

2. BREATHE - take a deep breath in through your nose, so deep that your belly expands, and then let it out very slowly through your mouth. You may have to take several deep breaths depending upon the situation. The purpose of this breathing is to calm yourself. (I've heard that the slower you blow out, the calmer the deep breathing helps you to be.)

3. THINK POSITIVE things to yourself like, "This person needs help", "It's going to be OK", "I can make it through this",

"Sometimes life isn't fair", "I'm a good person no matter what other people say or do", "Sometimes you get accused of things that you didn't do", "I'm strong", "I'm not going to make myself angry about this", "All I can do is try my best", "Sometimes you don't get what you want", "I can't control what others say or do", "I can't control who wants to be a strong friend", "I can do this", etc. (A disrespectful person needs help because being disrespectful doesn't help a person to have a good life.) Please remember the important fact that thinking negative things often leads to negative feelings and that negative feelings often lead to negative actions (like saying or doing something disrespectful).

4. SAY SOMETHING POSITIVE OR ASSERTIVE. OR SAY NOTHING AT ALL* -

Say something positive with a calm positive tone of voice like:

- "Wow, where did that come from?"

- "Whoa, that wasn't kind."

- "Oh my, bless you!"

- "Ooh, that didn't sound positive!"

- "Sorry, but we don't talk like that at our school."

- "Oh no, I'm sorry that you feel that way. Is there anything I can do to make things better between us?"

- "Oh, I'm sorry to hear that."

Or other **positive** statements that work for you (you fill in):

Say something assertive in a positive tone of voice, for example after someone makes fun of your shoes - you could say:

- "I guess you don't like my shoes - that's OK."

- "I like my shoes."

Be strong and refuse to let the imaginary arrows that others are shooting at you go through your armor and make you angry. Feel good about yourself by letting arrows bounce off of your armor.

Please don't say anything at all to someone who you don't know or to someone who you know is violent. It's not your responsibility to try to help them.

*If the disrespectful person says something like, "Don't tell me what to do" after you say something positive or assertive to them - you can choose to say nothing at all back or based upon the situation you might be able to calmly say something like, "I was just trying to help you." Do whatever you can to stay out of an argument that could lead to someone getting hurt.

5. WALK AWAY - run if you need to in order to get to safety. (Please keep in mind that many times, it's smart to be afraid. Please be careful if you have to run.)

A strong person regularly uses their shield throughout their life. With regular practice, using "My Shield" eventually becomes a good habit.

Many people feel that the best way to defend themselves is to be disrespectful to people who are disrespectful to them (in other words, shoot arrows back at people who shoot arrows at them). They call it "standing up for yourself." Unfortunately, I've seen many many times that standing up for yourself in a negative way by being disrespectful often ends with someone getting hurt, sometimes seriously. I suggest that using My Armor (p. 9) and along with My Shield to stand up for yourself in a positive way is a much better way to defend yourself than being disrespectful. It's not easy to learn to use these two things to handle disrespectful people in a respectful way, but it can be done if you practice using them daily. How do I know that this is true? I've seen students do it!

My Shield story #1: Even as a school counselor I need to use "My Shield" on a regular basis. In my office, I often hold mediations to calmly talk through and work out a problem between two students. One day a student was already sitting in my office and the second student came in and said in a grumpy tone, "What am I here for?" I felt like being grumpy right back by saying, "Well, you're here because you can't get along with people and this is the third time you've been here this week!" Saying what I felt like saying probably would have made the situation worse, and then she might have said something like, "Well, I'm out of here, I'm not doing this!"

Instead, I used "My Shield." First, I stopped and didn't have a quick response back. Next, I took a slow deep breath to calm myself. Then I thought to myself, "This young lady does not understand why she's here." I tried to say something positive by asking her, "Do you remember why Mr. W. (that's what I go by at school because it's easy for students to remember) ever wants to talk with you?" while at the same time putting my hands up in the air out to the left and to the right to form a "W" (with my head being the middle of the "W"). She didn't seem to remember, so I said, "Remember that I showed you the "W" with my arms

43

during a guidance lesson years ago - and it means that whenever I want to talk to you it's because I'm worried about you - and this girl here wants to find a way to make things better with you." Thankfully she calmed herself down, we had a good talk together, and they eventually signed a mediation agreement "to be polite and kind to each other at all times."

My Shield story - #2: A 7th grade student burst into my office, sat down quickly in the comfy blue chair and said, "I can't take another second with that science teacher, you have got to get me out of that class!" I had no choice but to go right to "My Shield". I didn't say anything right away. I took a deep breath in through my nose and slowly out through my mouth. I thought to myself something positive like, "I can help this young lady figure out how to get along with her teacher." I said something positive in a kind way as I looked her squarely in the eye. I said softly, "Yes you can!" She responded back with a desperate tone in her voice, "How?" - and then I knew that she was open to trying to make things work with her teacher.

I said to her something like, "Why don't we talk about exactly what a student is supposed to do when they go into a teacher's classroom?" So, for the next twenty minutes or so we developed this list:

1. Understand that the teacher is trying to help you to be successful and to one day get a good job that you enjoy doing

2. Greet the teacher by name as you come into the room

3. Talk quietly with the other students around you until the teacher starts to speak

4. Don't talk to or listen to anyone else during class unless the teacher gives you permission to do so

6. Give your full attention to the teacher, ignore distractions

7. Listen and try to understand what the teacher is trying to teach you

8. Raise your hand and ask a question whenever you don't understand something

9. Participate in class

10. Try to do your best on your classwork and complete it during class

11. Work well with others if you are assigned to groups

12. Refuse to goof around when working together in a group

13. Say goodbye to the teacher by name as you leave the class, possibly even adding "Have a good rest of your day!"

14. Complete your schoolwork and homework on time

15. Study for quizzes and tests

A week after this chat her teacher stopped me in the hall and said, "She's a completely different student, what did you tell her when you met?" I told her that I couldn't share the details, but that we talked about what she could do to be a better student.

About another week went by and I saw the teacher again in the hallway. She said, "You'll never guess what - she came to my room after school yesterday and asked me if I had anything I needed help with. I found something for her to do and she helped me for about a half hour!"

The high point of that school year was the end of the year awards ceremony. The science teacher went up on stage to the microphone and said, "I have a special award that I would like to read and then present to one of my students." She read, "Even though there were times during this school year when you and I had trouble getting along, I am presenting this award to you in appreciation of your efforts to get along with me and to become a better student."

Her student came up onto the stage and they both gave each other a big hug. I must admit that I got a bit teary when I saw this. I felt like I had been helpful to both the student and the teacher.

My Shield story - #3: I was so proud of one of our fourth graders a few years ago (and she was proud of herself also). She came to my office to tell me that she had used her armor and her shield to respond positively to a middle school student who had cursed her out on the street corner right after school the day before. After this happened, our fourth grader paused, took a deep breath to calm herself, and then said, "Oh, God bless you!" The middle schooler, who was fully expecting our fourth grader to curse her right back so that she would have an excuse to start a fight, said "What??" in a confused way. Our fourth grader then calmly and politely said, "Have a good day!" and walked away. She was strong by refusing to shoot an arrow back.

The Ring of Power™

All of us have this imaginary ring. Inside the ring are things that you have power over. Outside of the ring are things that you don't have power over.

Inside your Ring of Power is:

1. What you say
2. What you do - (this includes the hundreds of choices that you make each day - what you eat, what you wear, how much you sleep, how hard you work, how much time you spend with your family, how much time you spend reading, how much time you spend using electronics, etc.)
3. What you think (You can work daily on trying to think positively instead of thinking negatively. Please remember that thinking positive helps you and thinking negative doesn't.)
4. How you react (respond) to what others say, do, or think
5. Whether you make respect for your job, others, and yourself top priorities in your life
6. Whether you have a consistent positive attitude
7. Your anger (this will be explained in detail later in the book)
8. Whether you learn and then use the tools in this book daily

Outside your Ring of Power is:

1. What others say
2. What others do
3. What others think
4. How others react (respond) to what you say or do
5. Whether others treat you with respect
6. Whether another person wants to be a strong friend
7. Some things that happen to you (accidents, you or others getting sick or injured, losing your job, natural disasters, etc.)

Unfortunately, way too many people waste their time and energy being anxious, worrying, and/or making themselves angry about things that are outside of their Ring of Power. Specifically, they waste too much time getting themselves worked up about what disrespectful people say and do. On top of this, as you'll see in the next story, some people mistakenly think that they can get power over what disrespectful people say and do by threatening them with violence or by attacking them using violence.

Students who understand what's inside the "The Ring of Power" and what's outside "The Ring of Power" will find that it helps them as they try to use "My Armor" and "My Shield" daily.

The Ring of Power story: When I worked at the Alternative School (for middle school and high school students who had been thrown out of regular school), I had a student tell me that he wasn't going to take any more lip from another student named Juan - and that the next time Juan ran his mouth he was going to crack him upside the head. (In other words, he was telling me that he thought that he had power over Juan's mouth.) I asked him if he thought that hitting him would make Juan stop. He said, "Yes."

I paused and then asked him something like, "Juan's here at the Alternative School, how many times do you think that he's been cracked upside the head?" He thought about it for a few seconds and then said, "Maybe fifty times." I asked, "So, if he's already been cracked fifty times, what makes you think that when you crack him that he's going to stop running his mouth?" He said, "Oh, Mr. W., I'm really going to crack him." I said, "What are you talking about - knocking out his teeth, breaking his skull?" He said, "I don't know, whatever it takes." I asked, "What's going to happen to you if you really hurt him?" He shrugged his shoulders and said, "I don't know." I pleaded with him to not use violence to try to solve the problem. Thankfully he chose not to use it.

- **e**mpathetic - a strong person really tries to understand how others feel. In other words, they're able to put themselves in the shoes of other people (they can imagine how the other person might be feeling) and then take positive action to help.

Empathy story #1: When I was about four, I went to Firestone® with my dad who was having some work done on our car. While my dad was waiting in line at the service counter, I sat on a wooden chair along the back wall next to a large popcorn machine. The machine was coin operated which meant that when you put a paper bag on the chute and you put in a nickel, popcorn would come out of the machine and fill the bag. I could see the popcorn through the glass, I could smell the popcorn, and I wanted the popcorn. I was too young to realize that reaching up into the chute of the machine and trying to get popcorn was stealing.

I put my little hand into the chute, and I thought that I was close to getting some popcorn. But no, I couldn't reach any. As I started to pull my hand out, I realized I had a problem, I couldn't get my hand back out.

I had no choice but to call out to my dad for help. He spun around and came quickly to help me. He asked me to relax my hand and to pull it out slowly. I did what he asked, and I was able to get my hand out. He didn't yell at me. Instead, he gave me a hug, looked me in the eye, and kindly told me to not do anything like that again. My dad had empathy for me. I think that he was able to put himself in my shoes and understand that I was just a young boy who wanted some popcorn.

Empathy story #2: Here's a story about someone who showed me empathy big time when I was an eighth grader. The story begins way back when I was four years old. I was playing with my trucks on the floor and the phone rang for my mom. It was a school in a nearby town calling to offer her a job as a kindergarten teacher. She said, "I'm sorry, but I can't take the job because I have a four-year-old." They said, "Oh, that's not a problem, just bring him along." It wasn't a good thing having my mother as my teacher - sometimes I would call her mom by mistake and she would give me the "please don't call me mom" look.

I remember that we were served milk in small glass bottles with a paper cap for a snack. (This was before they started putting milk in paper cartons - I told you that I've been around for a while.) One day after we had just gotten our milk, the boy next to me dropped his bottle and it shattered on the floor. My mom looked right at me and said, "Jim, give him your chocolate milk and you go get a white milk." Even though I felt like saying, "Mom, he's the one who dropped his milk, why should I have to take a white milk?" I didn't say that because it would have been disrespectful to my mom.

Being the youngest and shortest kid every year in school made me the target of a few bullies up until ninth grade when I started to get taller. I usually tried to say something funny after I was insulted in order to get everyone to laugh and for it to be over. Several of my teachers thought I was the "class clown."

In eighth grade, the verbal bullying from one student turned into violence. Honestly, I didn't do anything to cause it to happen. One day after gym class while I was starting to get dressed in the locker room somehow without any adult supervision, out of nowhere Lucas (name changed to protect the guilty) pushed me really hard - so hard that I was flying in the air for a second, bounced off the bench that we sat on to get dressed, and landed on my tailbone and back. I was sprawled out on the floor against the lockers with a shocked "What was that for?" look on my face. Lucas just laughed and walked away. I didn't say anything to him or tell an adult about it. Thankfully nothing was broken.

Fast forward a few months later and I was in the lobby of the school waiting for my dad to pick me up after basketball practice. Wouldn't you know, Lucas was there too and again there was no adult supervision. Lucas came up to me and said, "C'mon Wegert, let's fight!" I was terrified because it was clear that Lucas could easily flatten me, probably with one punch. I didn't say anything. He repeated his request while at the same time lightly slapping me upside the face with one hand and then the other. He was cruelly taunting me.

Across the lobby was a boy named Tom (his real name in order to honor the strong), a guy I knew from elementary school even though we were never in the same class. He had empathy for me, he saw that I was in trouble, he understood how I was feeling, he put himself in my shoes - and then he took action in a positive way. He walked over to Lucas and said in a calm voice, "Lucas, he doesn't want to fight, could you do me a favor and leave him alone?" Lucas backed off and left me alone. In fact, he never bothered me again. Tom will forever be one of my heroes. (Tom used a calm request to get Lucas to stop bullying me. It was probably much more effective than giving Lucas a command - for example, yelling across the lobby, "Leave him alone!")

- **b**rave - a strong person is brave when they face danger or put up with pain without fear

Brave story: My dad and his brother-in-law, Uncle Willard, decided to go hit some golf balls for fun at a local park. They took my brother and me along to help pick up the balls so that they could hit them again. We were having fun until one of the balls went into a group of bushes. As I was looking for it, I accidentally stepped on a bee's nest that was in the ground. Suddenly bees were all over me, and I was stung at least five times. I remember one bee coming right toward my face and stinging me right above the eye. Ouch! (Please remember to "bee calm" when a bee is around you. If you try to swat at a bee to get it away from you, it may sting you because it thinks that you are trying to hurt it.)

Uncle Willard heard me screaming and he was there in a flash to help me. With no concern for himself, he quickly pulled my sweatshirt off to get the bees away from me. He was stung several times as he did this. He was brave. He saved me from being stung even more times.

But his bravery wasn't over yet. I made it back to the car while my brother, my dad, and Uncle Willard collected the golf clubs and the balls so that we could go home.

In the car I had another problem. Somehow a bee had come into the car and now I was trapped in the back seat of the car with it. I couldn't get out - because of the child-proof safety locks (these locks are designed to prevent kids from opening the backseat car doors while the car is moving). So, when I pulled on the handle of the door, nothing happened. Soon I started screaming and pounding on the car windows. I was in a panic.

Uncle Willard again came to the rescue. He opened the door and I yelled that there was a bee in the car. To protect me, he took his bare hand and squished the bee up against the glass - and by doing this, he was stung again. Uncle Willard was definitely my hero that day.

Having a positive attitude can really help a person throughout life. (By the way, the baseball acronym CCFFHREB stands for center, center, field, field, home, run, error, bunt - I know that one was a stretch to figure out - sorry about the corniness.)

Reflection: Do you think that the tool of "Attitude" can help you to build a good life? If so, why? If not, why not?

I can't emphasize enough that it's very important for everyone to understand that there's a direct connection between a person's thoughts, feelings, and behavior. For some reason, many humans often have negative thoughts, then have negative feelings, and then have negative (destructive) behaviors. If you really want to have positive (strong) behavior, you must practice every day thinking as positively as you possibly can. This will help you to have more positive feelings and having positive feelings will make it more likely that you'll have positive behaviors. Please keep in mind that negative thinking makes it less likely that you'll achieve your goals and dreams - and that positive thinking makes it more likely that you'll achieve your goals and dreams.

Here's an example of the difference between negative and positive thinking in a negative situation:

Negative situation: You earn your worst grade ever on a test

Negative thought: "I'm not a good student. I'll never be."

Negative feeling: sad, frustrated, angry

Negative action: stop trying to be the best possible student that you can be (give up)

Positive thought: "I can do better than this. This is never going to happen again. I'm going to work harder and ask for help."

Positive feeling: motivated, energized, determined

Positive action: put much more effort into trying to do your best in school, ask your teacher for advice about how you can become a better student and improve your test-taking skills

− (negative) thoughts usually lead to − feelings and often lead to − behaviors. + (positive) thoughts usually lead to + feelings and often lead to + behaviors. Please practice being + every day! (Strong people try their best to be + in − situations.)

NOTES:

5

RESPONSIBILITY

(Baseball acronym for the parts of this tool = HATS)

- for **h**andling pains in a positive way (a pain is a person who you have trouble getting along with, who you don't like, and/or who has been disrespectful to you)

I can almost hear you shouting, "But I don't want to handle people who are pains in a positive way - I want to get them back for what they've done to me." I understand and I have to confess that sometimes I feel the same way - but I've seen over and over again that handling pains in a negative way just doesn't help a person in the long run. It doesn't help a person to be successful and to have a good life.

Handling pains in a positive way is a skill that you're going to need throughout your life because you're always going to have some people who are pains in your life whether it's at home, at school, or at work. It definitely takes time to develop this skill - but you can do it if you really practice. Over the years I've seen many students do it.

It seems to me that there are three types of pains. The first one is someone in authority over you (parent/guardian, teacher, boss, etc.) who's telling you what to do or is telling you something that you don't want to hear. Some people make the bad choice to handle this type of pain in a negative way - by ignoring what's said, by doing what's requested with a grumpy attitude, by refusing to do what's being requested and/or by being disrespectful. The problem with handling this type of pain in one of these ways is that it doesn't help you to have a positive relationship with your parent/guardian, teacher, boss, etc. Not having a good relationship with these people can create big problems for you (bad grades, not getting a good job, not getting promoted, getting fired, etc.)

The second type of pain is someone who's a classmate in school or a co-worker at work who you know isn't violent. These people can usually be handled in a positive and assertive manner. For example, if this type of pain says something like, "Where'd you get that shirt?" in a negative way - you could possibly look them right in the eye and say calmly and politely, "I guess you don't like it - that's OK" and walk away. If they keep giving you a hard time about the shirt, just say something like, "I think it looks good" in a positive way and then walk away.

Please keep in mind that when you try to handle a pain at school or at work in a positive and assertive manner, it needs to be done carefully. Please never be disrespectful - it doesn't help them or you (please remember to use My Armor and My Shield).

The third type of pain is someone who you know is violent or someone who you don't know. As much as you feel like saying something negative or smart to a person after they have been disrespectful to you, please don't do it. Please be strong and instead just completely ignore the person and walk away - run if necessary. (Acting like you didn't even hear what they said while walking away is often a good strategy.) Following this suggestion could one day save you from being attacked and badly injured. (If you're a high school or college student and don't believe this, please see the self-control of the body stories on pp. 156-160.)

If you're still not convinced that learning how to handle pains in a positive way is really important, please consider this - one of the main reasons that people get fired from a job is that they can't get along with other people. And what's the reason they can't get along? - that's right, it's because they've never learned how to handle pains in a positive way.

Handling pains in a positive way story - Sometimes it helped me as a kid to try to be humorous by making myself look bad. Way back something really rude that bullies did was whisper in my ear, "You stink." I would turn it into a joke by smelling my armpits one at a time and saying, "You're right, I should have put on more deodorant!" Everyone would laugh and it was over. I didn't really care if people laughed at me because I knew that I was a good person even if I was being laughed at. Their arrow just bounced off of my armor.

- for **a**lways trying to make a good choice

I realize that this is very difficult because we're faced with so many choices daily. When students ask me, "How do I make a good choice when I'm under so much peer pressure to make a bad choice?" - I usually say something like, "Imagine that the person who loves you the most and who's strong (as defined on p. 3) is sitting on your shoulder whispering in your ear what the good choice is in a particular situation. If you do what you think they would tell you to do, almost always this will be a good choice." A person who remembers to do this when making choices will gradually make more and more good choices. They'll eventually become so strong as a person that they'll almost always make good choices. They won't really care about the negative things that disrespectful people say, do, or think about their good choices, and they won't be too concerned if disrespectful people don't like them because of their good choices. One of the reasons that they feel good about themselves is because they always try to make good choices.

(Another way to make a good choice in every situation is to ask yourself the question, "Does this choice respect my job, others, and myself?" If the answer is "no" to any of these three questions, please don't do it.)

An example of a good choice is choosing to put in the effort daily to practice being a strong person.

Choices story #1: A 16-year-old who worked for me as a camp counselor during the summer at a "Y" camp, died when his so-called friend decided to try to get away from the police after a minor traffic violation. I could be wrong, but I think that it was going through a stop sign without stopping. His friend lost control trying to go around a curve and hit a tree. My counselor, who wasn't wearing a seat belt, horribly went through the windshield and died. He left behind his devastated parents, sister, friends, and co-workers who loved him so. He was an awesome guy whose smile and personality lit up a room whenever he walked in. I cried more than I ever have at his funeral. (Please don't ever try to get away from the police.)

Choices story #2: Here's a story about when I made one bad choice after the other. These choices could have caused my friend to get really hurt or worse. I mentioned earlier that I lived just across the street from a ravine when I was a child. One day someone in the neighborhood got the bad idea to dump their grass clippings over the edge of the ravine at the back of a large vacant lot instead of taking the time to bag them. Soon many people started doing it and I decided to do it too. (I made the bad choice of following the crowd.)

One day, just after I'd finished cutting the grass, I saw my friend Corky (that was his nickname) in front of his house, and I waved him to come over. I asked him if would help me dump the grass clippings over the edge of the ravine because the box was big, heavy, and hard to handle. He was a strong friend.

Corky helped to steady the box as it sat precariously on the rusty red Radio Flyer® wagon with a partially broken handle that I was pulling. We made it across the street and then we went on the path through the vacant lot to the edge of the ravine. When we got there and looked over the edge, I saw a little tree about twenty feet down with a burlap ball on the bottom of it - which meant that it could easily be planted. I said to Corky, "I'm going to get that tree and plant it in my yard." Corky said, "I don't think that's a good idea." Did I listen? - no.

I made it down about eight feet, slipped on the wet rotting grass and tripped over a root in the ground. I fell forward and somehow, I tucked in my head as I started rolling head over heels down the side of the ravine. After rolling for what seemed like 30 seconds, I came to a complete stop with a jolt. When I opened my eyes I saw a huge cloud of dust, I was covered with dirt from head to toe, my arm hurt from banging it as I rolled, and my ear had a cut on it.

When I looked up, I could barely see Corky's head as he looked down trying to see me. I had fallen about 50 feet and now I was sitting on a ledge about 20 feet above the creek. I yelled, "Corky!" He yelled back, "Are you OK?" I yelled, "I'm OK, but please go call the Rescue Squad (which was a special small fire truck with ropes and other things needed for a rescue). Just as Corky started to leave, I yelled, "Corky, come back!" I was worried about making a big scene and having everyone in the neighborhood know that I fell down the ravine. I yelled to Corky, "Forget about the Rescue Squad, please just go get my parents." I thought that maybe they could rescue me. He started to leave and then I yelled again, "Corky, come back!" I was worried that my parents would be mad at me for making the bad choice to go and get that little tree. I yelled, "Corky, could you walk down the ravine using the path to see if I can get down from where I'm at?" He said, "OK." Thankfully the path nearby wasn't too steep.

It took him about five minutes to get down to the bottom of the ravine and now he was directly across the creek looking up at me. He said that there wasn't any way for me to get down. Did I accept that answer? - no. I asked him to cross the creek and be right under the ledge where I was stuck to see if there was any way for him to help me get down. He made his way across the creek by walking on large rocks, but when he got under the ledge, he still said that there was no way for me to get down. I moved slightly by accident and a few small pebbles fell on his head. For some reason, as a 10-year-old, I thought that this was funny. Corky didn't say anything. Then I moved a little bit on purpose and more pebbles fell on his head. Corky said, "Hey - knock it off!!" Did I listen? - no. I moved again and much to my surprise the entire ledge collapsed, I went flying over the head of Corky, I landed hard on my tailbone on the bank of the creek, bounced, and ended up with my legs in the water.

I turned back and saw Corky's face. It was pale, it kind of looked like he had seen a ghost. I felt bad about what I'd done. I made one bad choice after another, and my final choice could have caused my friend to get hurt or even killed (a large rock could have been in that ledge, and it could have crushed Corky's head). He was kind as he helped me to get out of the water and he walked with me back to my house. I went in and took a shower. I didn't tell my parents about these bad choices until years later.

The good thing about this scary event is that it helped me to learn how important it is to try to make a good choice in every situation and about the importance of listening to a strong friend who is trying to help you make a good choice.

Choices story #3: In 8th grade we got a new bus driver, and to begin with she seemed like a nice person. Things were going well until some students started trying to ride a bus that their friends were on instead of the bus they were supposed to be on. This bad choice caused some buses to become overcrowded. To solve this problem, the school district decided to issue paper bus passes that had to be shown each day in order to get on the bus.

For several weeks every day I showed my bus pass to the bus driver as I got on. One day, just as the bus was approaching, I realized that I forgot my bus pass and that it was too late to go back home to get it. As I stepped on the bus, I explained to the bus driver that I forgot my pass. She said firmly in a not too pleasant tone, "Get off!" I was surprised and I tried to plead my case, "You know me, I've shown you my pass for weeks." She repeated her command.

I got off the bus and went home. Thankfully my mother wasn't angry, and she dropped me off at school on her way to work.

The situation with the bus driver kept getting worse and worse. Almost everyone didn't like her. One day things came to a head. At school a student made a poster which read, "Please help us - we're being held captive by a power-hungry bus driver!" and snuck it on the bus. He sat in the back seat and showed the poster to people in cars behind the bus. Someone got the bad idea to shoot spitballs using small pieces of notebook paper that were formed into a ball with spit and then using the barrel of a clear Bic® pen to launch them toward the bus driver. Several people started doing it. Things were really getting out of control, but no one had the strength to tell anyone else to "stop and knock it off." The final straw was when someone decided to use a rubber band to shoot paper clips at her.

The bus was driving on a boulevard (a road with two lanes going in each direction with a grass median strip in between) when the bus driver realized that some students were shooting things at her. When we got to a traffic light, she quickly made a U-turn back to the school. The bus quickly went from being loud and rowdy to dead silence.

When we arrived back at the school, she opened the bus door, looked at us and said, "Y'all just stay right here, I'll be right back!" Then she stormed into the school.

Soon she came back to the bus with the assistant principal, and he asked her to point out which students had been giving her trouble. She pointed toward the back of the bus and the assistant principal said, "Ok, Wegert, let's go!" My life passed in front of my eyes. I breathed a big sigh of relief when the bus driver said something like, "No, not him, it's the guy behind him."

I learned from this experience that it's very easy to sit back and do nothing when other people are doing things that aren't right. I should have been strong enough to tell the guys, "Things are getting out of hand, we need to stop before something really bad happens."

Choices story #4: I had a "friend" named Justin (name changed to protect the guilty) who had a real problem with his driving. Whenever there was a situation that called for caution, he for some reason would always speed up on purpose. For example, if the street was narrow and only had barely enough room for two cars going in opposite directions to pass each other safely, Justin would speed up to force the other driver to move over or to stop completely so that a crash wouldn't happen. At the time, I thought that his driving was kind of exciting and I didn't realize how he was putting both of us in danger of getting hurt in an accident.

One day, I was with him as he drove down the same boulevard that I just described in the last true story. He was tailgating a person who was driving in the left-hand lane - too slowly for him. He asked me if he could pass on the right. I looked behind us and said, "Yes." He changed lanes quickly and stomped on the gas. He didn't realize that a light was coming up soon until I yelled, "The light!" Right after I yelled, I saw a white Cadillac starting to pull slowly into the intersection. Justin slammed on the brakes hard and his car started to skid sideways. We were so close that I saw the fearful eyes of the man in the Cadillac that we were about to hit.

62

Luckily, we missed the other car by about six feet. Justin said, "Oh - bad word", threw the car quickly into reverse, backed right into a fire hydrant, and put a huge dent in the back bumper.

As we started driving again, he asked me if I had time to go with him and swing by the middle school to pick up his brother. I told him, "No, I've had enough driving for today, please take me home."

He dropped me off and then he went to pick up his brother. He turned off the car at the middle school and waited for him. When he tried to start the car again to drive back home, it wouldn't start. In fact, it had to be towed to the repair shop and then to the junkyard because it was too expensive to fix. He ruined his parent's car due to reckless driving.

I decided that day not to repeat this bad choice and I never went driving with him or accepted a ride from him again. When he asked me, "Why not?" - I think I told him, "Sorry, but after what happened last time, I don't feel safe driving with you."

Choices story #5: I regularly tell my students that it's very important to do whatever you can to get along with your siblings. I explain to them that they'll probably have a relationship with their siblings here on earth longer than they will with their parent or guardian. I encourage them to have such a good relationship with their siblings that if one day they need to call and ask for help to solve a problem, the sibling will say, "What can I do to help?" instead of saying, "Well, that's not my problem!" and then hang up.

I've been blessed with a wonderful brother - my only sibling. He's really smart, earned great grades, was a starter on the team that won the league championship in basketball as a senior in high school, went to prestigious universities, has had several high-level professional positions in business and now teaches chemistry in high school - but the most important thing to me is how well he's treated me over the years.

I know this is going to sound hard to believe, but I can't remember a time when he was unkind to me unless I completely deserved it.

One of those times was after he was told by my mom, as she was leaving the house, to tell me to unload the dishwasher. When he told me to do this chore, for some reason, I decided to give him a hard time. (Can you imagine a little brother doing something like this? I can almost hear you yelling, "Yes!!") I think I rudely told him "No!" He said that I need to do it because mom will be back soon. I decided to irritate him on purpose by unloading the dishwasher really slowly - like I was in slow-motion. I'd slowly take out one dish after another and put each one slowly into the cabinet. I think that I was smiling as I did this to be even more irritating. He told me to stop messing around and get to work. Did I listen? - no.

For some reason, I don't know why, I made the bad choice of taking a wooden cutting board from the bottom rack of the dishwasher and throwing it at his leg. It hit him just above the ankle and the chase around the house was on. It didn't take him very long to catch me, pin me to the ground, and turn me on my side so that my left shoulder was facing up. He then wound up and punched me hard in the shoulder. I learned the lesson that day that it's not a good idea to irritate your brother on purpose. He was kind and never said a word about what happened to my mom when she returned home.

When I tell my students about my brother, they seem amazed because one or more of their siblings are disrespectful to them pretty much every day. I try to give them suggestions of what to say to a sibling who has just said something disrespectful to them (use "My Shield") - for example, "Wow, that's not how a brother is supposed to talk to a sister." Usually, they tell me that if they say this, their sibling will say, "I don't care!" I then ask my students what they can say that's really positive to a sibling who just got up into their face and said, "I don't care." They often say, "I would just say that I don't care either!" I ask them with a smile in my voice, "Whoa - would saying that be positive?, that kind of sounded like an arrow, would saying that help you to have a better relationship with your brother?" They chuckle and say, "I guess not." I then try to help them come up with positive things to say like, "Well, I care. I want us to have a good relationship." or "I'm sorry to hear that." I encourage them to not get into arguments with their siblings and to calmly walk away if one starts.

Choices story #6: When I was in fifth grade there was a kid named David who thought he was "all that." One day in the hallway he asked me to pretend to hit him in the jaw. Since I didn't want to make him unhappy (I made the bad choice of being a "people pleaser"), I went along with what he requested, and I didn't make any contact. The whole thing was a setup. He recoiled after my fake punch and acted like I hit him in the mouth and told everyone that I had loosened the cap on his tooth. He also told me in front of his friends that he was going to beat me up after school for doing that. I asked him, "What are you talking about? - I didn't do anything to your tooth." He didn't say anything back.

Another student was strong enough to tell our teacher that there was a big problem and that a fight was going to take place after school. She tried to make things better between us (we didn't have a school counselor back then) - but it didn't work. For some reason, David was determined to have a fight with me. The teacher debated about who to send home first (we all walked home) and she decided, much to my relief, that it was better for me to go home first and that she would hold David for 20 minutes after school to make sure that a fight didn't happen.

65

What she didn't realize was that David had told his "friends" to be waiting for me outside of school. As I left in a hurry, several of them grabbed me and held me. They told me that they were going to hold me until David came out so that we could have a fight. Thankfully a few six graders nearby saw what was happening and told them to let me go.

I never ran home so fast in my life. I may have even set a record for a mile run for a kid my age without even realizing it. I kept looking over my shoulder to see if anyone was after me.

When I got home panting, no one else was home because both of my parents were at work and my brother wasn't home yet. I remember struggling to open the front door with my key and to lock the front door behind me because my hands were shaking. I was worked up and panicky even after I was inside the house.

I kept looking out the window and soon a group of about ten kids, including David, was on the front sidewalk of my house chanting together, "Wegert come out!" They knew that I was home because one of them saw me peek out the window. The crowd wanted to see a fight. One guy even used a Magic Marker® and a piece of notebook paper to make a little sign which he held up for me to see. It read, "COME OUT!" All of the people chanting were making the bad choice of encouraging a fight.

I didn't come out. I was surprised at school the next day because David and all of the rest of the guys acted like nothing had happened. (I think that David was just trying to blame me for loosening the cap on his tooth - maybe so that he wouldn't get into trouble at home.)

I learned that day that none of the guys who were outside my house were strong enough to make a good choice and be a strong friend to David. (A strong friend would have said to him, "This isn't right, Wegert doesn't want to fight. Please just leave him alone and let's all go home.")

- Strong people make the good choice to stay out of other people's business. They don't do things like listening in and/or getting involved in other people's conversations, telling other people what they've heard (gossiping), spreading rumors, etc. These things may be interesting and exciting for a short time because of the drama that's created, but they create conflicts and waste valuable time. If you do these things, you may develop a reputation as a person who has the bad habit of being in other people's business. In other words, being in other people's business doesn't help you to have a good life.

- for **t**aking care of yourself

The American Academy of Sleep Medicine® has recommended that students 12 and under sleep between nine and twelve hours a night and students age 13 and up sleep between eight and ten hours a night. The reason for these recommendations is that lots of things are going on inside a person's body as they grow up, so they need more rest than adults who are fully grown.

A person who takes care of themselves also eats a balanced diet including fruits, vegetables, breads, cereals, lean meat, and fish. They don't eat sweets, potato chips, and other "junk food" in large amounts. They don't overeat (remember that it takes about 20 minutes for the stomach to send a message to the brain that the stomach is full, so it's important to eat your food slowly and chew thoroughly). They choose to eat some foods that they don't really like because they're good for their health. They eat a good breakfast every day, one that minimizes sugar - whether they feel like it or not - unless they have a medical condition that prevents this. (Breakfast is the most important meal of the day because it's been so long since the body has had food.)

A person who takes care of themselves has good personal hygiene - they bathe regularly, and they brush their teeth carefully for at least two minutes twice a day (at least before or after breakfast and before bed). They also floss their teeth once a day.

People who take care of themselves also don't do anything that could harm their body. Sadly, the list of things that a person can do to harm their body is long. Many of these things are enjoyable for a short period of time, but they can cause damage. Regardless of what anyone else says or is encouraging you to do, choosing to harm your body or changing how your brain works with alcohol or other drugs is a bad (disrespectful) choice. (If the people you hang with are making bad choices and/or are encouraging you to make bad choices, please get away from them and find some strong friends to hang with.)

And finally, people who take care of themselves exercise on a regular basis if approved by their doctor. The most important part of exercise (after you stretch and warmup) is getting your heart rate up to its target heart rate zone for at least twenty minutes straight three or more times a week. The internet has information about how to calculate the target heart rate zone for your age. **(Please be sure to talk to your doctor before starting any exercise program.)**

- for serving others

May I suggest that the first group of people a strong person should serve is his or her family, relatives, and friends. He or she can serve them by offering to be of help whenever needed. A strong person also serves others by doing something that helps the community in which they live. Usually this involves some type of volunteer activity such as volunteering at an after-school childcare program, serving in school club or a community service organization, joining a group that has adopted a highway by picking up litter monthly, offering to rake leaves or shovel snow for free for an elderly neighbor, etc. Serving others helps a person to get their focus off themselves and on to other people (that's where the real joy is).

Reflection: Do you think that the tool of "Responsibility" can help you to build a good life? If so, why? If not, why not?

A person of peace never uses the popular excuse, "He or she disrespected me", for hitting someone. Instead, he or she realizes that whether someone respects you is outside of your Ring of Power and that your value as a human being has nothing to do with whether others respect you (remember you're a miracle, no matter what others say or do).

Please keep in mind that many people who say or do disrespectful things are just trying to start a problem. Sadly, they enjoy having problems with others because they think it's exciting and it makes them feel good about themselves. Some are hoping that you'll say or do something disrespectful back so that they have an excuse to start a fight. Please refuse to fall into the trap that they're trying to set for you. Please be strong and be a person of peace.

I tell my students that I'm trying to help them get their armor thicker and thicker - so thick that they let anything disrespectful people say just bounce off.

Many students are more concerned about being respected by others than they are about trying their best in school. They don't seem to realize that being respected by others is outside of their Ring of Power and that trying to be the best possible student is inside their Ring of Power.

"Learn from the mistakes (bad choices) of others. You can't live long enough to make them all yourself."
- Eleanor Roosevelt

NOTES:

6

EFFORT

(Baseball acronym for this tool = E)

A strong person gives their best effort in everything they do. They're known as a hard worker. They believe that anything worth doing is worth doing to their best ability. They take pride in the fact that they always try to do their best even when their best isn't as good as someone else's best (because they realize that everyone has different levels of ability and skills - and that's OK). They know that giving their best effort will make it more likely that they'll have a good life.

More specifically, giving your best effort will make it more likely that you'll:

- do well in high school and get financial assistance and/or scholarship money to go to a trade or technical school, a two-year college, or a four-year college

- do well in trade or technical school, a two-year college, or a four-year college and get a good job that you enjoy doing instead of a bad job that you don't like

- do well in your job

- eventually get promoted to a better job

- attract a hard-working strong person to date one day - if and when you decide to date

A big part of effort is perseverance. You know, sticking to something and not giving up. Some people are only willing to give their best effort when what they're doing is easy and/or enjoyable. They often just give up when they don't feel like doing something and/or if it's difficult for them. A person with perseverance never gives up and keeps working hard even when they don't feel like it. If they get discouraged, the discouragement doesn't last - they take a break and then quickly get back to work. They finish what they start.

Effort story #1: I didn't really understand until 6th grade that harder work usually results in better grades.

Mrs. Hall, my favorite teacher of all time (sorry Mom), caught my attention one day when she announced that anyone who got all of the answers correct on every spelling test during a marking period would get an "A" in reading.

I knew that earning an "A" would make my mom really happy, so I accepted the challenge. I studied how to spell the spelling words of the week and their definitions more than I had ever studied anything before. Each week, when I got all of the answers correct, it kept me motivated to keep working on the next set of spelling words. I ended up getting all of the answers correct on all of the tests and there it was on my report card - my first "A" in reading.

Near the end of 6th grade, Mrs. Hall mentioned a word that we had learned earlier in the year. She asked, "Does anyone happen to remember the definition of that word?" I raised my hand, she called on me, and I gave her the right answer. She smiled and said, "We're going to have to nickname you The Human Dictionary." Her comment made me feel proud.

Unfortunately, I didn't work as hard as I should have all the way up until 12th grade and because of that, I just barely made it into a really good school, Miami University in Ohio. I didn't qualify for any scholarships to pay for college because my grades were not high enough. (Please don't make this same mistake.)

I worked harder in college than high school, but my grades in my first year of college were not good.

I knew that I had to start doing things differently if I wanted to earn the grades that I needed to be able to get a good job after graduation. So, I decided to stop studying in my dorm where I lived because other guys would interrupt my studying by periodically knocking on my door to ask if I wanted to do something. I also stopped studying in the main library because other students were talking way too much instead of studying. Thankfully, I found a small library in a small building on campus where people who really wanted to study went. It was like heaven. I can remember that students who left the library were careful to close the library door slowly to make sure that the door didn't bang and disturb anyone as they left. I also found empty classrooms in academic buildings on campus where I could hide and have a quiet place to study.

It took me three years of extra hard work to pull my grades up to a "B" average by the time I graduated. These grades helped me to get a decent job soon after graduation.

Effort story #2: My mother was a great teacher for over 30 years including 22 years at Millridge Elementary School in Highland Heights, Ohio and her expectation was that everyone, regardless of their ability, would work hard and do their best in school. One evening she had a conference with the parents of a 4th grade girl who was getting all A's. When she showed the parents their daughter's report card, they were all smiles. My mother proceeded to tell them that there was a problem. One parent asked, "How could there be a problem? - she's getting all A's!" My mother said, "Unfortunately the problem is that your daughter is lazy - she's earning 92% or 93%, just enough to earn an "A." If she really worked hard, she could be earning 97% or

98%. This story has a happy ending. When this young lady had the opportunity as a senior in high school to nominate the teacher in her life who had the biggest influence on her - she nominated my mother, and my mother received an award at the school district awards banquet. My mother's dedication as a teacher helped this young lady become an outstanding student through hard work - instead of just being an excellent student. My mom helped her to have a good life.

Effort story #3: When I was about eight, I started playing in a boys' baseball league. We weren't very good, but we played hard every game no matter what the score was. Our team was "Little Rock" and we played "Atlanta" in our most exciting game. Both teams came into the game without a win in the first four games of the season. I came up to bat in the bottom half of the last inning with two outs and a runner on second. Our team was trailing 6-5. I swung and missed the first two pitches that were right down the middle. I remembered that my dad had told me to always swing instead of taking a called strike three. I was laser focused on the next pitch, which once again was right down the middle, and I carefully made sure to put the bat on the ball. I hit it and I think that it went into the gap between the left and center fielder and rolled all the way to the fence. I was paying attention to my first and third base coaches as they moved their arms in a circle to indicate that I should keep running. The tying run scored and as I went to third, the throw from the outfielder flew over the third baseman's head and hit the fence in front of the Atlanta bench. I wanted to go home, but when it hit the fence, it was out of play.

Gary, our one power hitter, was up next. I was ready to run on contact. He hit the ball right back to the pitcher and the pitcher threw it to first base as I ran home. Somehow the first baseman dropped the ball, and we won the game 7-6. I was buried under a pile of joyous "Little Rock" players. Our coach was really happy too, but he apologetically told us that he didn't have time to take the team to Dairy Queen® after the game. He said that he would take us the next time we won.

Unfortunately, that time never came, and we never went to Dairy Queen® because our team finished with 1 win and 15 losses. Even with all of those losses, I was really proud of our team because we always tried our best, we always cheered for each other, and we never gave up - no matter what the score was.

Effort story #4: Whenever I would get my report card my mother and I would sit down to look it over (as a school counselor I've been amazed over the years about how many students don't have any idea what their grades are).

If I had too many "C's", I knew what was coming - no TV for the entire next marking period (and by the way, back then personal computers, video games, cell phones, etc. didn't exist).*

If I met my goal for the marking period, then we would do something special like going out for dinner, going bowling, etc.

After we talked about if I had met my goal, we would set a new goal for the next marking period, focusing especially on the main subjects - reading, math, science, and social studies. The goal we set was always higher than the grades I just earned. She consistently pushed me to work harder and to do my best.

*I never had two bad marking periods in a row.

Effort story #5: When I was talking to a 7th grade student, who was having problems getting along with other students, I asked her to consider putting in the effort required to become a strong person who has respect for others. She seemed to laugh off my suggestion as something that wasn't very important. She didn't seem to realize that the reason I was asking her to work toward the goal of becoming a stronger and stronger person every day wasn't for her parents, it wasn't for her teachers, it wasn't for her friends, - it was for her. (Over the years I've learned that people who put in the effort required to become a strong person and to stay a strong person are much more likely to have a good life.)

Effort story #6: When I was going to college for my first master's degree, I decided to coach a boys and girls under age 12 softball team in the summer for fun. We weren't very good, but we worked hard to improve. One day we played a team that was really good, but several of their players were disrespectful to our team with their words and actions. Their left fielder was particularly rude. One inning he decided to turn his hat around backwards because he was sure that we didn't have anyone on our team who could hit a ball all the way out to him. I must admit that I had great joy when our female first baseman hit the ball over his head during that inning for a triple.

The best player on our team played center field. I told him to be sure to back up the left and the right fielder whenever a ball came their way - just in case they missed it (which happened a lot).

About halfway through the season before the start of practice his mother came up to me and told me that her son had decided to quit the team. I told her that the team needed him, and I asked if I could try to talk him out of it. She said, "No - he's tired of losing all the time."

Looking back now at what his mother said to me - I should have politely suggested that she tell her son in a kind but firm way that he made a commitment when he joined the team to play the entire season, that it's important to learn to keep your commitments, that it wasn't right for him to just quit in the middle of the season and let down his team members who looked up to him, and that if you let him quit now, you're teaching him that it's OK to break your commitments when things don't go the way you want them to go.

Effort story #7: As I mentioned before, I was short for my grade. In fact, I played guard on the school basketball team in 8th and 9th grade. In 9th grade I pretty much only played when we were being blown out. I was fouled late in one game and went to the free throw line to shoot one and one. The cheerleaders were about to do the "Up in the air, over the rim, come on Jim and put it in - sink it!" cheer, but before they started the cheer, I heard one of them ask, "What's his name?" I shot my first free throw and it bounced around the rim and fell in. My next shot, the highlight of my season, was nothing but net!

I tried out, but I didn't make the team in 10th grade. I grew quite a bit, maybe close to five inches, over the next two years. I went to a new high school in 12th grade, and I decided to try out for their team. I practiced a lot on my own during the summer doing basketball drills at a park nearby and I ran around my house, with my dog Gretchen, our beloved beautiful vizsla running with me, to get myself into playing shape even before the tryouts started. When tryouts began, I was pretty rusty but gradually the rust started to wear off and I thought that I had a good chance of making the team since I was now one of the tallest guys.

One Monday, the coach told us that we were going to be traveling to play a scrimmage on Friday against you know who - my old high school! I was really excited about being able to show those guys from my old school, who thought that they were *so* good, how much better I'd become. My excitement quickly fizzled when the coach announced which players would be going on the trip. I wasn't invited, in fact even some of the 9th graders were invited! I was really demoralized - and I decided to make the bad choice to give up and quit trying out.

I saw the coach about a week after I stopped going to tryouts and he asked, "Where have you been?" I told him that since I didn't get invited to the scrimmage that I didn't think there was much hope for me to make the team. He asked me to meet him after school in the gym. We sat in the bleachers and talked about things. The team manager was handing out practice jerseys and he asked the coach if he should give me one. The coach said "no." It was painful. He tried to make me feel better by telling me that I would be the first person to be put on the team if someone got hurt. Unfortunately, this didn't happen even though a few people on the team never played at all because of football injuries.

I was pretty hard on myself, asking myself, "After all of that work, why did you just give up and quit?" and "Why didn't you just tell the coach how important it was for you to play a few minutes in that scrimmage and to ask him to cut you right after the scrimmage if you didn't do well?" If I had just forgotten about the scrimmage and had decided to use not being invited as fuel to motivate myself toward excellence - maybe I would have made the team. I was beating myself up over it.

My dad was kind and gave me a new pocketknife in recognition of my efforts to make the team.

Over the years I've thought about this quite a bit and I wish he would have said before I quit something like, "You're not quitting - you're going to give it everything you have, and if they cut you, then we're going to have a "cut party" with pizza to celebrate your efforts."

You may not believe it, but this bad choice to quit trying out sticks with me to this day. I know it sounds crazy, but after all of these years I periodically still have a dream that I'm trying out for that team. In my dream I'm playing great, I'm driving in and scoring as well as knocking down long shots from the outside. I'm playing better than I ever have. Then somehow in my dream I start to wonder if the coaches are going to notice that I'm a lot older than the guys I'm trying out against. Then I wake up and realize that it was just a dream.

The good news from this quitting experience is that I learned to never "grow weary" and to never quit trying to do what I can to help make the world a better place - a world filled with respect.

(Wouldn't you know, I think the year after I graduated our team did really well. That's the team that I probably would have been on if I hadn't started school at age four. Oh well, the fame of being on that team probably would have just gone to my head.)

Reflection: Do you think that the tool of "Effort" can help you to build a good life? If so, why? If not, why not?

"After the work's done right, it's time to have good clean fun."

NOTES:

7

SELF-CONTROL

(Baseball acronym for the parts of this tool = BATM)

- of the **b**ody

Way too many people don't know how to control their body by only using violence when absolutely necessary for self-defense. Since movies, TV, video games, and other things in our popular culture make using our bodies to hurt other people seem OK and even exciting - many people don't understand how important it is to be strong by being a person of peace and that violence is evil. (What else can you say about something that has injured or killed so many people?) When I say evil, I'm talking about violence itself - not the people who use violence. (I may be naïve, but I believe that some good can be found in anyone.)

Self-control of the body story #1: Occasionally a fight breaks out on the playground during recess at our elementary school. Thankfully no one has been seriously hurt on the playground during my seven years there. Unfortunately, after a fight I often hear that right before the fight started there was a group of students surrounding the students who were about to fight, chanting "fight, fight, fight." If I find out who these students are, I call them down to my office as soon as possible - not to get them into trouble, but to try to help them. Even though I'm feeling angry that one of my students would do such a thing, I try to have a polite and kind discussion with them about why this isn't right. I ask them if they would have done this if their mother was right there with them, I ask them how they would have felt if someone had been seriously hurt or even killed in the fight - a fight that they encouraged to happen. I ask them to never to do this again.

81

Instead, I ask them to be strong and be a peacemaker, a person who encourages people to talk out their problems (maybe with my help if needed) instead of having a fight. I ask them to become a person of peace.

A person of peace never says or does anything to start or to encourage a fight. They never shoot arrows like, "What are you going to do about it?", "What's up?", "Make me.", "Go ahead and hit me.", "Your momma", "Let's fight.", "I'll meet you in the bathroom or on the corner after school so that we can fight" etc. They don't agree to fight anyone anywhere regardless of what names they're called or even if their mother is insulted. (Please remember that anyone who insults your family is really screaming "I need help!")

If someone asks a person of peace if they want to fight, they say "no" and walk away. They ignore the disrespectful things that people say to them after they refuse to fight. They choose to stay out of arguments because they know that arguments often lead to violence. If someone attacks a person of peace for no reason, they only use self-defense (self-defense = using only enough force to get the person off of you, to be able to get away from the person, and to get to a safe place).

Self-control of the body story #2: My conversations with students who have a problem with regularly trying to use violence to solve their problems usually go something like this:

Student: "You've got to be ready to fight at any time in order to keep your reputation and to survive."

Me: "Hmm, when I look out the window of my office, I see lots of students outside who don't get into fights - how are they surviving?"

Student: "I dunno."

Me: "What eventually happens to people who try to use violence to solve their problems?"

Student: "They go to jail?"

Me: "Possibly. I've found during all of my years of working with young people that a violent person eventually either breaks someone's head or worse and goes to the juvenile detention center/jail - or they get their head broken or worse."

Student: "Those things aren't going to happen to me."

Me: "How many times do you think that I've heard that?"

Student: "Lots of times."

Me: "Yes, hundreds of times."

I then bring out newspapers and briefly read articles about teenagers who were seriously injured or worse from violence.

Me: "So many of these people also thought - that's not going to happen to me."

Me: "Do you realize that all it takes for you to get hurt badly is for you to slip, to be off balance for a second, for the other person to hit you just right, and then you fall and hit your head? - and that no matter how tough you are there's always going to be someone out there who's tougher."

Me: "Do I have to visit you in the juvenile detention center/jail after you hurt someone badly or visit you in the hospital after someone hurts you badly and for us to share a cry for you to learn that violence doesn't solve problems?"

Self-control of the body story #3 (Caution - graphic): A few years ago, a group of girls who were participating in an elementary school after-school program that involves running, asked their teacher if they could go to the bathroom before they went home. The teacher said "OK" and unfortunately two of the girls in the group got into a big argument in the bathroom that even included cursing. All of the girls left the building except one of the two who had been in the argument. When the last girl came out, a small group of girls were still standing outside. Someone in the group pointed and yelled, "There she is!" She made the really bad choice of encouraging the girl who just came out to go and fight the other girl.

They ended up chasing each other back and forth across the road until one of them was hit by a car. Thankfully she turned her hip toward the car just as it hit her. People were screaming "call 911!" I was there in less than a minute. The guy driving the car that hit her was standing in the middle of the road, frantically trying to call 911. He was shaking as he tried to dial the numbers. There was big dent in his car, but he didn't care about that. He had just accidentally hit a person. It was a horrible situation.

Luckily the girl didn't break any bones and she only missed about a week or so of school. The only thing that saved her from a more serious injury was the stop sign that's located near our school. When I tell my students that they can die from an argument, some don't believe me until I tell them this story. It's more real to them because it happened at our school.

Self-control of the body story #4: In eighth grade, on a day that we had a substitute teacher for homeroom, I failed to control my body and almost got into big trouble. If you can believe it, back then the school didn't have video announcements, everything was over a loudspeaker. I was trying to listen to the announcements, but a guy in the row right behind me, Jon, was talking loudly when he wasn't supposed to. I wanted to listen to the announcements because I needed to find out when tryouts for the basketball team were going to be held. I asked Jon politely if he could talk more quietly so that I could hear the announcements. He didn't listen - he may have even talked louder. I said to him firmly, "Jon, I'm trying to hear", while at the same time I tapped him very lightly on the side of his cheek with my open hand at the same time trying to get his attention. I got his attention alright.

He stood up quickly and punched me right in the mouth. I punched him back. The substitute quickly intervened - but I had a real problem. The force of the punch pushed the inside of my lip hard against the metal braces on my teeth, and I couldn't get my lip off the braces. I mumbled to the teacher, with my mouth closed, that I needed to go to the bathroom quickly to solve the problem. This is going to sound really disgusting, but when I got there, I had no choice but to peel my lip off of my braces over the sink. It hurt pretty bad, and my lip was bleeding a lot.

Of course, we were both immediately sent to the office. Back then the consequence for fighting was three swats on the bottom with a paddle by the assistant principal. As we walked into his office, Jon's hair was all messed up and I was holding a brown paper towel (like the ones that we still have at our school today) on my bleeding lip. Since we'd never been in trouble before, the assistant principal had mercy on us and said, "By the looks of you two, I think that you've learned your lesson - you can go back to class." We said, "Yes, we have - thank you!" and went back to class.

The next day our regular homeroom teacher was back. She was furious. She said something like, "How dare you get into a fight on the day that we have a substitute?" She moved our seats to opposite sides of the room.

That day I learned to never put my hands on anyone in any way - even lightly tapping someone on the cheek to get their attention (except when absolutely necessary for self-defense and then only using enough force to get the person off of you and to get away).

(A strong person also controls their body in other ways. My wholesome book about dating for teens and young adults, *True Love Lasts,* addresses this subject.)

- of **a**nger

First of all, let me clear up a fairy tale that I hear from my students almost every day. They tell me that "so and so made me angry" and/or "I have an anger problem that I can't control." They don't seem to believe me at first when I explain to them that there's no such thing as someone else making them angry.

Self-control of anger story #1: I try to prove this by asking them to imagine that they're having an argument with someone at home. I simulate the argument by using my hands pointing at each other, moving the fingers of each hand and making an angry "wa,wa,wa" voice back and forth between the two hands. Then I say to imagine that the phone rings and they calmly and politely answer by it saying, "Hello, may I ask whose calling?", instead of yelling angrily into the phone "wa,wa,wa,wah!" They laugh. I then ask my students the question, "If other people make you angry and you can't control it, how in the world could you go from being really angry one second to calmly talking into the phone the next?"

I also say **(not to K-2nd grade students, Caution-graphic)**, "I hope that this never happens, but let's imagine that you've been in a car accident, and you're hurt really bad (broken leg, broken arm, broken skull, and internal bleeding) - so bad that you're lying in the hospital after surgery and the doctors have to give you medicine to put you into a coma, so you won't move

86

around and everything can heal. When you're in a coma, you can't see, you can't hear, you can't feel, and you can't think - you're just floating along in la la land (my students chuckle when I say this) - and a person who you say "makes you angry" comes into the room and says and/or does the exact same things that you say 'make you angry', and maybe even kicks you or lightly slaps you in the face - would you be angry?" My students almost always say, "Yes!"

I say, "No, actually you wouldn't be angry (they're surprised when I say this), because you wouldn't even know what was happening - remember you can't see, hear, feel, or think when you're in a coma. You would eventually wake up, the person would be gone, and you wouldn't remember anything.

I then tell them that this proves that we make ourselves angry when we see certain things with our eyes, when we hear certain things with our ears, when we feel certain things with our sense of touch, when we think certain things - and (snapping my fingers) just like that we make the bad choice to make ourselves angry - and since we have done it so many times before in our lives, we truly believe that someone or something other than ourselves makes us angry.

If the student still doesn't think that they can control their anger, I ask them if they could control their anger for the rest of the school year if I promised to give them a brand-new car filled with $100,000 in cash. Almost all my students say, "Oh, yes!" To build the excitement, I tell them that we would have their car out in the school parking lot, it would probably be a convertible so that we could see the cash spread out in the back seat, and a big banner would be put on the side of the school with their name on it declaring that this is their car and cash if they control their anger for the rest of the school year. I also say that we would have armed guards watching their car 24/7 and that we would light up the parking lot with huge spotlights at night so nothing would happen to their car and cash.

I then ask them, "I bet you don't think the car and the cash are really there, do you?" They always say, "no." I then say to them, "You're not going to believe it, but they're actually there - you're young and you don't see them because they're in the future. I illustrate the point by using the table in my office and two pens. I tell them that the long side of the table represents life all the way from birth to death. About six inches in from the left-hand side I place the first pen and say, "You're about ten-years-old and this pen represents where you are on the road of life. Because you're young, your small car has headlights that only shine a short distance into the future, maybe as far as what you're doing this weekend."

I then place the other pen about six inches from on the right-hand side of the table and say, "This pen represents Mr. W's car. Mr. W. is much older than you and his car is big and it has strong headlights like a lighthouse, and they shine way into the future. I can see that if you learn to control your anger, be kind, work hard, and graduate from high school, you'll make at least $300,000 more over your lifetime (I say this while gradually spreading my hands apart along the side of the table to help them understand that I'm talking about the entire time that they'll be working during their life) than if you don't graduate from high school, that you'll make at least $450,000 more over your lifetime if you graduate from a 2-year college, a trade school or a technical school than if you don't graduate from high school, and you'll make at least $600,000 more over your lifetime if you graduate from a 4-year college than if you don't graduate from high school."

So, then I say, "So, let's just take the graduating from high school compared to not graduating from high school example. If you make $300,000 more over your lifetime, could you buy a new car and still have $100,000 left over? They say "yes" and then I say, "Yes - you could probably buy 2 or 3 cars and still have $100,000 left over."

And finally, I ask, "The question is do you want to learn how to control your anger, be kind, and work hard to one day get the car and the cash?" You'd be surprised at how many students say "yes" after this explanation. I tell the students who say "yes" to feel free to wave me over when they see me in the cafeteria and whisper in my ear "I'm going for the car and the cash." I also tell them not to be surprised if I see them acting the fool and I whisper in their ear, "Are you still going for the car and the cash?" (When I ask this and they say "yes", I say, "Then you better settle down and get to work.")

It really brightens my day when I see one of my students in the hallway or on the playground after school and the first thing that they say to me is, "Mr. W. - I'm going for the car and the cash."

Self-control of anger story #2: I tell my students that if they make themselves angry because of what someone else says or does, they're giving their power away to the other person. In other words, they're letting the other person control them in a negative way - which is not a good thing. I tell them it's like they're a remote-controlled car, and the other person is holding the controller and pushing the buttons to control them. Some of my students can see that they are allowing disrespectful people to control them, and they make the good choice to work on not letting this happen - by staying positive and using My Armor as well as My Shield.

So how does a person control their anger? The first step is to understand that we make ourselves angry as just described. The next step is to realize that we all carry around an imaginary big yellow anger barrel with us (kind of like the barrels that toxic waste is kept in). The anger barrel of some people has hardly anything in it, but the anger barrel of other people is near the

89

top. When the anger barrel of a person reaches the top, the person either oozes (the person is grumpy, irritable, or depressed) or explodes (the person yells, curses, throws things, punches a wall, hits or kicks others, etc.). Sometimes people just ooze, sometimes people ooze and then explode, and sometimes people just explode. Different things make people fill up their anger barrel quickly - for some people it's an insult, for me it's when someone tells me something that I know for sure is a lie.

One way to control your anger is to use "My Armor" (described in detail on pp. 9-10). Here's a recap: Imagine when another person says something disrespectful to you, when they insult your family, when they roll their eyes at you, when they make fun of you, when they give you a dirty look, when they suck their teeth, when they laugh at you, when they talk about you behind your back etc. - they're really just shooting an imaginary arrow at you.

To make sure that you're not hurt by an arrow (and make yourself angry after the arrow hits you because they're painful), you need to remember to put on your imaginary metal armor, just like a knight wears, as you get dressed every morning - so that when their arrows hit you, they just bounce right off - boing! They bounce off because you're *so* strong (your armor is *so* thick) that you don't really care about what disrespectful people say, do, or think. You refuse to let them have power over you and how you feel about yourself.

I realize that making yourself angry from what disrespectful people say or do is a very tough habit to break - but it can be done if you practice every day.

As you put in the effort required to stop making yourself angry about what disrespectful people say or do, please keep in mind that it's likely these people will get even more disrespectful when you don't get angry. The reason for this is that they're desperately trying to get what they want - an angry reaction from you. I explain to my students that giving a disrespectful person an angry reaction is like "giving them candy." It's "candy" because some people think that trying to make other people angry is fun and seeing people get themselves worked up is entertaining. It's going to take a large amount of effort to constantly ignore them.

If you don't give in by being disrespectful back to them, eventually disrespectful people usually move on and find someone else who they can get worked up. (If they don't stop, please ask your school counselor for help.) I counsel my students to not give out "candy" - because giving it out only encourages more disrespectful behavior in the future.

A key to controlling your anger is to find ways to drain it daily. People can drain their anger safely in different ways, for example:

- taking deep slow breaths - in through your nose and very slowly out through your mouth while saying positive things to yourself (in your head) like, "it's going to be OK", "I can make it through this", "sometimes life isn't fair", "everyone at times gets accused of doing something they didn't do", "this is not worth getting angry about", "this person needs help", etc.

- counting to whatever number you need to count to in order to cool off

- going for a walk around the block or around the office (or at school down to the school counselor's office if you have permission from your teacher)

- exercising

- listening to music

91

- squeezing something (like a stress ball) and then releasing it very slowly before squeezing it again

- going to your room to scream into a pillow

- going down to your basement to scream or yell (make sure to get permission beforehand so that people in the family know what's going on and won't get scared) - some people find that it helps to also march in place while moving their arms and legs (like they're running) at the same time to release more anger

- forgiving (not because the other person is sorry or because they deserve forgiveness, but because it helps you drain your anger barrel - and that helps you to not become an angry person)

- of the **t**ongue

The tongue may be the biggest thing that keeps people from becoming a strong person.

Some people think that since we live in a free society, they should be able to say pretty much anything they feel like saying. Well, the problem is that just because we have the right to say almost anything, doesn't mean that it's a good choice (a choice that takes you toward your long-term goals and is right).

People who don't know how to control their tongue (use it wisely) are less likely to have healthy relationships. Millions and millions of people have damaged or destroyed relationships with others, don't get the job they wanted, or don't get the promotion they wanted - because they said something without thinking first, spoke disrespectfully to someone, or because they talked behind someone else's back.

When you're a strong person, you don't have an unkind word to say to anyone about anything no matter what they say to you.

You remember that every person is a miracle. You handle people who are pains in a positive way. (If they don't want to have a good life, that's up to them.) If you mess up and are disrespectful to someone - you apologize if possible, learn from your bad choice, forgive yourself, and then go back to trying to be strong.

Many people think that refusing to say something disrespectful back to someone who has said something disrespectful to you is a sign of weakness. May I suggest that it's actually a sign of strength. It's a sign that you realize that everyone deserves respect even if they don't give it to you just because they're a human being. It's a sign that you fully understand that anyone who is being disrespectful to you is really saying "I need help" - and that saying something disrespectful back doesn't help them or you.

Self-control of the tongue story #1: Unfortunately, some of our elementary school students really need to work on using their tongue to say only kind words to others (in other words, they need to work on not shooting arrows). Also, a good number of students don't use My Armor and My Shield when someone says something unkind to them as much as they should - instead they just tell the teacher. This gets to be a bit much for teachers and some of them have asked me if I could help these students break this habit.

So, I developed a guidance lesson for students to teach them when they're supposed to tell the teacher about something that happens. They're supposed to tell the teacher when they're threatened with violence, or when they are pushed, kicked, tripped, hit, etc. - as well as when they hear someone else being threatened with violence or they see someone else being pushed, kicked, tripped, hit, etc. In other words, they only tell when they are unsafe or someone else is unsafe. Other than that, they're supposed to be using My Armor and My Shield. (We stress to students that the reason that should tell is not to get the other

93

student in trouble. The reason they should tell is because they want to help the other student get their behavior under control and they want everyone to be safe.)

But sometimes a student is saying or doing something that's unkind, and they don't stop even after another student has asked them kindly to do so. This is when we teach them to use "The Four I's"™. The Four I's are: "**I**'ve asked you kindly to stop, if you don't stop, **I**'m going to have to tell the teacher, **I** don't want to, but **I** need you to stop." If the student still doesn't stop, we teach our students to go up to the teacher and say something like, "Mrs. Strong, James has been kicking the leg of my desk again and again. I've given him The Four I's, but he still won't stop." (The teacher then steps in to help the student solve their problem and to help James get his behavior under control.)

Self-control of the tongue story #2: One day after school I was sitting in the kitchen eating my snack before starting my homework and the kitchen phone rang. My mom answered and said out loud, "Hello - Mrs. Lina (my fourth-grade teacher), how are you?" while giving me the "why is your teacher calling me" look at the same time. She repeated what Mrs. Lina told her so that I could hear, "You're having problems with my son - Oh, he's talking all of the time without permission - I'm *so* sorry. Mrs. Lina are you crying? What else is he doing? He's also telling jokes to get other students to laugh and they're not paying attention to what you're trying to teach. I'll have a talk with him. Please let me know if he causes you any more problems." She hung up the phone, looked me right in the eye, and asked me, "Am I ever going to get another phone call like that?" I said, "no." And thankfully, she never did.

Hearing this story helps my elementary school students to know that I too had problems controlling my tongue at their age - and with practice they can break that bad habit.

Self-control of the tongue story #3: A few years back, a really sharp 3rd grader raised his hand during a guidance lesson and asked a question. He said, "Mr. W. - how come it's so easy to say something mean (disrespectful) and so hard to say something kind after someone has been mean to you)?" I wanted to give the class a chance to answer his question, so I said, "Wow, that's a great question. Class, does anyone have an answer?" They came up with several good ones including: 1. We're mean back because we're trying to defend ourselves. 2. We mistakenly think that if we're disrespectful back to someone, it will make it less likely that they'll be disrespectful to us in the future. 3. We want to get back at the person who was disrespectful to us (revenge). 4. It's hard to be kind when you've made yourself angry. 5. We do it because it's a bad habit.

- of their **m**oney

Many people have never been taught how to control money. They earn or are given money, but it goes through their fingers quickly because it's spent too fast on "stuff" that they don't really need. Please read at least one book about how to control your money using a budget that includes saving for the future. (Your librarian can give you a suggestion based upon your age and there's a suggested book for older students on p. 170.)

So far, you've learned about the five tools of a strong person and their parts. The next section of the book discusses how to use the tools to build a good life by respecting your job, others, and yourself.

Reflection: Do you think that the tool of "Self-Control" can help you to build a good life? If so, why? If not, why not?

"Live life with emotion, but don't let your emotions control you."

As they grow up, most children learn to be controlled by someone outside of themselves - for example, by parents, school staff, and peers who tell them what to do or influence what they do on a regular basis.

Unfortunately, when a child doesn't learn how to control themselves (to have self-control) by the time they're 15 years of age, they often spin out of control when these outside controls are removed (for example, when they graduate from high school and go on to post-secondary school or move out of the house - and they can do whatever they want to do whenever they feel like doing it). Many can't handle the freedom of not being told what to do or being influenced all the time by someone else. Many don't consider doing their best in school or at their job, respecting others, and taking care of themselves as top priorities - and sadly they often end up messing up their lives.

Also, children who don't develop self-control are more likely to become "people pleasers." This type of person repeatedly chooses to make bad choices in order to fit in and be liked. People who put in the effort required to develop self-control are more likely to be strong enough to try to make good choices in every situation and to have a good life."

SECTION 3: HOW TO USE THE FIVE TOOLS TO BUILD A GOOD LIFE

Q. Is there any such thing as good anger?

A. Yes, anger that has a good purpose or that helps another person is good anger. For example, a mother who yells at her son and tells him to "get inside the house right now" after he started to step into the street without first looking both ways, is displaying good anger. She's trying to teach her son to cross the street safely. She wants him to look both ways and to cross the street only at a traffic light or a stop sign with a crosswalk so that he doesn't get himself badly injured. Bad anger is an attempt to emotionally hurt the other person or to get your own way. It's disrespectful and selfish.

"A bad choice takes you away from achieving your long-term goals. A good choice takes you closer to achieving your long-term goals."

"A person who always tries to make a good choice in every situation is much more likely to have a good life than a person who doesn't."

8

WHAT SHOULD I DO NEXT?

It's not going to be easy - but important things rarely are

Now that you know what the five tools of a strong person are, you may be wondering what to do next. Here are a few suggestions:

1. Believe that these tools can help you become a strong person (if you're not one already) and that you can use these tools to build a good life.

If you need some encouragement, please keep in mind that many people are in the process of learning the tools, using the tools to build a good life for themselves, or they're helping their children to develop the tools that they need to build their own good life. Please check out the latest posts and comments on the Respect Club blog which can be accessed through the respectclub.org website. Hopefully reading a post or a comment will encourage you to keep trying to be strong every day (and if you post a comment about how you had respect for your job, others, or yourself - possibly it will encourage someone else to keep trying to be strong). Please be sure to only use your first name when making a comment. (All comments are approved before they're published on the blog. Comments with identifying information, other than first name and state or country will not be published.)

2. Make becoming a stronger and stronger person every day one of the main goals in your life. Not just an "I'll work on it whenever I feel like it, goal" but an "I'm going to do whatever it takes, no matter how hard it is or how long it takes, goal." I'm still working on this goal every day. (Becoming and remaining a strong person is a lifelong process.)

Some people decide to keep this goal uppermost in their mind by rating themselves every day from 1 to 5 based upon how many tools of a strong person they feel that they used well during the day.

They ask themselves five questions:

- Did I display good character today?

- Did I have a positive attitude today?

- Did I fulfill my responsibilities today?

- Did I give my best effort today?

- Did I have self-control today?

If they didn't display one or more of the tools, they think about why and they think about what they could have done differently.

Other people find it helpful to start a journal where they write down what they did each day that was strong. (They can even post it right away as a comment on the Respect Club blog.) Over time they're able to see the progress that they're making. (Some people find it very helpful to work together with a strong friend toward the goal of becoming a strong person. You can hold each other accountable for words and actions and you can encourage each other to make good choices.)

3. Practice every day being strong. Specifically, if you're not already doing it, start practicing using your tools - having good character, displaying a positive attitude, fulfilling your responsibilities, giving your best effort, and demonstrating self-control. Please keep in mind that learning to be a strong person is just like learning a sport or learning to play a musical instrument - the more you practice, the better you get. At first,

it's probably going to be hard and you're still going to make some bad choices. Please remember that it takes a while to break old habits, like being disrespectful back to someone who's been disrespectful to you. When you say or do something that isn't strong - pick yourself up, dust yourself off, apologize if possible, try to make up for what you said or did if possible, learn from your mistake, forgive yourself, and then go back to trying to be strong. Please never give up!

In the next three chapters, we'll look at suggestions of how to use your tools to respect your job, others, and yourself.

"A person who is loving, caring, and giving - and who tries to put the needs of others first by getting off of themselves, is more likely to have a good life."

"A strong person is modest. They don't have a big head and think that they're better than anyone else. They realize that everyone has things that they need to work on to improve - including themselves."

"Be strong and embrace optimism – in other words, try to find the good in everything and believe that things can get better."

NOTES:

9

HOW TO USE YOUR TOOLS TO RESPECT YOUR JOB

This is important - you might be working 40 years - do want to be in a job that you don't like for 40 years?

When you respect your job (which for many people reading this book is to be a student*) you:

- make respect for your job one of the top priorities in life

- realize that being a student and having the possibility of one day getting a good job that you enjoy doing is a great opportunity that millions and millions of children around the world would give almost anything to have. (Unfortunately, some children in poor countries don't even have a school to go to and if they do, it's nothing like your school. Some schools only have a dirt floor. The roof of the school is made up of sticks held together with tar to keep out the rain. Their teacher never went to college like yours did. She uses a large paper tablet and a Sharpie® marker to write information for her students to see instead using a fancy electronic board like your teacher does. But even in these bad conditions, every student is completely focused on the teacher. They wouldn't even think about not having respect for their job, or others. They know that their only hope of escaping poverty and having a good life is to get a good education.)

- take advantage of this great opportunity by working really hard in school

- realize that school isn't free - even though it seems like it is. Every household and every business in your community pays taxes that are used to run your school. Your job is to make yourself, your parent/guardian, your teacher, and the taxpayers proud by doing your best (remember that everyone's best is different - for some it's all A's, for some it's A's and B's, for some it's B's and C's, for some it's C's and D's). Please don't cheat yourself and make it less likely that you'll have a good life by not doing your best.

- treat everyone in your school or in your place of work with respect (like I said before, don't have an unkind word to say to anyone no matter what they say to you or say behind your back, don't gossip, don't spread rumors, don't talk behind the backs of others, and stay out of other people's business)

- get along well with others and work well with others as a team (even with others who you don't particularly like)

- don't be easily offended

- be very slow to make yourself angry

- always look for ways to improve your job performance (For example, if you're a student, after each marking period ask your teacher for suggestions of how you can improve your grades - especially your grades in reading and math. If you have a regular job, every three months or so you ask your supervisor for suggestions about how you can improve your job performance.)

- take the suggestions for improvement from your teacher or boss and put them into action

- ask your teacher for extra help before or after school if you need it. This shows your teacher that you really care about doing your best and earning the best possible grades. (In college, in order to pass a really hard math class, I went to extra help Monday through Thursday evenings - and still only earned a "C".)

- display character (be honest in all things, have integrity by doing what you say you are going to do, show that you can be trusted)

- have a positive attitude (cheerful, caring, friendly, forgiving, and respectful). Be one of the most positive people at your school or at your job. Please don't be a complainer. It's easy to complain, but a person with a positive attitude finds the good in a bad situation and takes positive action, if possible, to make things better.

- fulfill your responsibilities at school and at work the best you can. When you feel frustrated, take a break, ask for help if you need it, and then get back to work. Persevere - never give up! (Shockingly, unfortunately only one student in all my years as a school counselor has answered, "Yes", when I've asked them the question, "Are you doing your best in school?")

- understand that giving your best effort in your job will really help you both now and in the future (for example, moving up to the next grade, graduating from high school, a trade school, a technical school, a two-year college, a four-year college, being promoted to a better job where you currently work or getting a better job somewhere else)

- exhibit self-control (you control your tongue even when you don't feel like it, you control your anger and calm yourself down when you're feeling angry)

- ask your classmates or coworkers when you need something from them (make a request) instead of telling them to do something for you (giving them a command). Most people respond much better and more quickly when they're given a request. Do this even if one day you have a job where you're the boss.

Respect your job story #1: To encourage my 3rd and 4th grade students to respect their job, I teach them about the Career Roller Coaster™.

I stand at the front of the class holding my left arm bent at a 45-degree angle using my hand held straight and flat as an extension of my arm. I explain to them that my arm represents the first big hill of the Career Roller Coaster, and that the tip of my middle finger of my left hand represents 12th grade. I then use my right hand to show them where their roller coaster car is on the hill (3rd grade is about a fourth of the way up from my elbow).

I tell them to notice (as I slowly move my right hand up the hill while keeping my left arm and hand stationary) that as they go up the hill, school gets harder as they move from grade to grade - and that they need to be prepared to really work hard to keep respect for their job as one of their top priorities in life.

Next, I tell them that the Career Roller Coaster isn't like a regular roller coaster where there's only one track when you get to the top of the first hill (12th grade). I explain that if they respect their job and give their best effort as they go up the hill - when they get to the top, they'll see that there's more than one track.

In fact, the more they respect their job from 3rd through 12th grade, the more tracks they'll see when they get to the top. After they graduate from high school, they'll get to pull a lever on their roller coaster car and make it go on the post-secondary school track that they chose to go on.

I keep my left arm and hand in the same position, and I move my right hand in a downward motion from the top of the hill as I show them each track. I say, "One track could be going to a trade or a technical school after high school, another track could be going to a two-year college after high school, and yet another track could be going to a four-year college after high school." I let them know that the better they do in 3rd through 12th grade, the more choices they'll have, including the choice of which post-secondary school or college they'll go to.

I also tell them if they respect their job during all those years, it's more likely that they'll receive financial assistance and scholarship money, so they'll be able to afford to go to the post-secondary school of their choice. Finally, I let them know if they continue to do their best even in post-secondary school, it's likely that one day they'll be able to get a good job that they enjoy.

Respect your job story #2: Way back when I supervised all aspects of a YMCA® sleepaway camp, one of the rules for the camp staff was, "there's no complaining allowed." The reason for this rule was to help keep staff morale high throughout the summer. I remember sitting in the dining hall eating dinner during camp staff training before camp started and hearing the camp director (who was a teacher during the school year) say to her staff in a loud but very pleasant voice, "Oh! I think I might have just heard a complaint, but that couldn't be, because we don't complain here at Camp Shand!" I think that the staff member who she heard complain said, "Sorry!" The director said something back like, "That's OK, I just wanted to remind everyone about our rule." The camp director was able to communicate her expectations to the staff in a positive manner and the staff ended up doing a great job of creating wonderful lifelong camp memories for the campers that summer.

Respect your job story #3: I have some students who make themselves angry when their teacher tells them what to do or tells them to stop doing what they're doing. When a student complains to me about this, I explain to them that their teacher is just doing their job - and that they have been told by the principal to tell their students what to do. I also explain to them that unless they own their own business and they're the boss, they will always have a job with a boss who tells them what to do.

*Please refer to the story on pp. 44-46 about how to respect your job as a student.

NOTES:

10

HOW TO USE YOUR TOOLS TO RESPECT OTHERS

Respect for others helps both them and you

When you respect **o**thers you:

- make respect for others one of the top priorities in life

- love on your family and make them feel special

- display character in your relationships (you're honest all of the time, you have integrity by keeping your word, you show through your words and actions that you can be trusted)

- truly care about others

- take the time necessary to really listen to others

- have empathy for others

- don't have the me, me, me (selfish) attitude

- realize that every person is a miracle who deserves respect (even people who you don't like or don't like you)

- show that others are important by what you say and do

- don't say or do anything disrespectful to others (regardless of what they say or do to you)

- are friendly to others

- are willing to be a strong friend to others who are looking for a strong friend

- are kind to everyone (even to people who are put down by others and even to people who are unkind to you)

- are helpful to others

- try to lift others up by giving them compliments and/or encouragement

- use your cheerful attitude to brighten the day of others (even when you don't feel cheerful - fake it when necessary - no one likes to be around a grumpy negative person)

- handle pains in a positive way (as described on pp. 55-57)

- stay out of other people's business

- are not too concerned about whether or not people at your school or your job like you or treat you with respect - because you know that you can't control these things. (You're wise and you know that you're a good person regardless of what others say or do.)

It may be hard to believe but trying to show respect for others at all times can really help both them and you. Specifically, it:

- makes it more likely that you'll be able to get along with just about everyone

- makes it more likely that one day you'll be promoted to a better job

- often makes a bad situation better

- makes other people feel good and feel important

- is a positive example to others (it might even help them to become a more respectful person)

Drama story: A good number of students seem to be more interested in being involved in the drama at school than they are in being the best possible student. I tell my students that drama is like a huge whirlpool of water that's spinning round and round with lots of things going on. Looking at the whirlpool, standing on the outside edge, it seems so exciting - gossip, rumors, who likes who, who said what to who, etc. Many people can't resist the temptation to put their toe into it (get involved with drama) and suddenly they find themselves quickly and completely pulled in. Being in the whirlpool of drama takes up so much time and mental energy that they don't have the time and energy that they need in order to be the best possible student. I also warn my students that being in the whirlpool could eventually cause them or someone else to be emotionally and/or physically hurt.

"If you step into a real whirlpool of water, it can drag you down and pull you under. Stepping into the whirlpool of drama in school or at work can do the same thing and cause you all kinds of problems."

"All of a sudden, I realized that being in the drama wasn't helping me. So, I decided to ignore people who say mean (disrespectful) things to me and to stop listening to people who were just trying to start drama. I pulled myself out of the drama and focused on having a few strong friends and my schoolwork. It was a good choice."
- an eighth grader

Some students, who are trying to become a strong person, choose to think of themselves as an actor who has a role to play in their own movie. Their role is to respect their job, others, and themselves. They know that by trying to play their movie role every day, it's more likely that they'll have a good life.

NOTES:

11

HOW TO USE YOUR TOOLS TO RESPECT YOURSELF

When you respect **y**ourself you:

- make respect for yourself one of the top priorities in life

- take care of yourself as explained on pp. 67-68

- realize that taking care of yourself makes it more likely that you'll be in good health and that you'll recover more quickly if you become sick or injured (many people make the really bad choice of not being too concerned about their health - until they lose it)

- realize that you're a miracle and that you have a lot to offer this world

- love yourself - but don't have a big head and act like you're better than other people

- admit, apologize, and try to make up for your bad choices

- aren't too hard on yourself when you fail to be strong - instead you learn from your bad choices, forgive yourself, and then go back to trying to be strong

- keep in mind the five tools of a strong person (character, attitude, responsibility, effort, and self-control) as you try to respect yourself every day

- minimize the use of electronics (before you shoot an arrow by rolling your eyes in disgust about this statement, please hear me out)

Over the years as a school counselor, I've learned that many students spend way too much of their valuable time using electronics of all types. This waste of time can have devastating effects such as:

- not doing their best in school

- not being awarded financial assistance and scholarship money so that they can afford post-secondary education (a trade school, a technical school, a two-year college, or a four-year college, etc.) because their grades are not high enough since they haven't put in the time required to be the best possible student

- not getting the rest that their body needs to be healthy because they're up until all hours of the night using electronics

- mental illness (research shows that excessive use of electronics is not good for mental health - it can lead to things like anxiety, depression, eating disorders, etc.)

- becoming addicted to electronics

Electronics story: Many students, especially students who are not doing well in school, have told me that they're not addicted to their electronics. I usually say, "That's great. Why don't you prove that by telling your friends that you aren't going to use any electronics for two days in a row and then stay off of them." Most students say, "I don't feel like doing that." I could be wrong, but I think that the reason they say this is because using electronics has become such a big part of their lives that they can't even imagine a day without them - and that the use of electronics is their main source of entertainment. I don't hesitate to tell my 4th grade students that I've never met a person in their twenties who says, "I wish I would've had more time using my electronics in

114

4th grade", but I've met lots of people in their twenties who say, "Man, I wish I would've spent more time trying to be the best possible student when I was young because since I didn't, now I'm stuck in a bad job that I don't like."

- the excessive use of electronics is causing people to have weak face-to-face communication skills

Face-to-face communication skills are needed by everyone to communicate well throughout their lives.

In order to have the best possible communication, both people in a conversation need to be able to see each other so that they can fully understand the words and feelings that are trying to be communicated. Studies show that only 35% of face-to-face communication is verbal and the remaining 65% is nonverbal (facial expressions, body language, etc.). The only way for a person to fully develop their face-to-face communication skills is to practice talking with others face-to-face on a regular basis.

So how does a person force themselves to practice? A suggestion is that they consider turning electronics off completely during a specific time of the day (and let their friends and relatives know that they're doing it, so they won't be worried) - and then find someone to have an uninterrupted face-to-face conversation with during that time. (Please see pp. 143-146 for more information about good communication.)

Social media story: When my children were younger, we had a rule at our house - we don't post anything that's negative on social media. We told them if we found out that they were posting negative things, they would not be allowed to use our network any longer. During my years as a school counselor, I've dealt with many problems caused by students using social media in a negative way. It's been both shocking and saddening to read what students have said to each other over social media that they would have never said in person or if their parent was with them. Being negative on social media often leads to conflict, sometimes violence, and almost always regret.

I realize that becoming a strong person may sound like an impossible task, something that's overwhelming - kind of like being asked to eat an elephant.* So, when my students seem overwhelmed when they think about trying to become a strong person, I ask them the question, "Can you eat an elephant?" All of them say "no!" I cheerfully tell them, "Oh, yes, you can!" With surprise they ask, "How?" I say, "One bite at a time!" You can become a strong person (and stay one) if you practice being strong each day. Every day is a new challenge. You can do this!

*No elephants were harmed in the writing of this book.

A special note about electronics to parents: Please consider following the screen time (TV, video games, tablet, computer, phone, etc.) recommendations by age of the American Academy of Pediatrics® which can be found by searching on "aap recommendations for screen time."

Also, please consider delaying when your student gets their first smartphone. I wholeheartedly agree with the Wait Until 8th™ movement that encourages smartphone use be delayed until at least 8th grade so that your student can fully experience childhood without the negative influence of a smartphone. Information about this movement can be found at waituntil8th.org.

If you decide to purchase a smartphone for your student so that they can communicate with you when necessary, may I suggest that you consider buying a basic phone with only a basic plan that allows your student to receive and make calls, text, and take pictures - a phone that has no data, no apps, no ability to download apps, and no ability to access the internet.

If your student already has a smartphone, my respectful suggestion is that you have the passwords to their social media accounts so that you can monitor if they're using them in a positive and safe manner. They may not be happy about it, but the health and safety of your student outweighs your student's right to privacy in this situation.

It's not easy being a firm, fair, kind, and consistent parent in today's world. Hang in there and thank you for all that you do to help hold our society together!

"Sadly, the companies that make phones, video game consoles, computers, tablets, or the latest electronic gadget could care less if you mess up your life by putting things that aren't good for you into your mind and by wasting massive amounts of your time instead of spending it to work on your top priorities in life. In fact, these companies actually design their products to make them addictive so that people will use them more. The same goes for social media. They just want your money."

Respect - Just Give It!™

"I don't need rewards for doing my work and being nice to other kids. My reward is learning."
- comment from a 3rd grader (Is this a strong comment or what?)

SECTION 4: OTHER IMPORTANT "STUFF"

NOTES:

12

HOW TO MAKE LEMONADE OUT OF YOUR LEMONS

Everyone is going to have lemons in their life

When I talk to my students about their problems, I often refer to problems as lemons. I ask them, "What does a person's face look like when they bite into a lemon?" They tell me that their face looks all scrunched up and they look grumpy.

I explain that unfortunately during their life they'll have small, medium, large, and extra-large lemons. For example, a small lemon is something like you spilled your milk this morning and made a mess. A medium lemon is something like you're sick in bed for three days in a row. A large lemon is when you get older you have an accident driving and you put a big dent in your car. An extra-large lemon is something like you or someone else has a very serious or even life-threatening health problem.

I go on to explain that it's not possible to go through life without having any lemons - so it's very important that you learn how to turn your lemons into something good.

I then ask the student what's something good that you can make using lemons. It may take a few guesses, but eventually they guess "lemonade." We talk about how lemonade is made and they sometimes forget that "sugar" is one of the ingredients needed to make it.

I explain that "sugar" is looking for something that's good in a bad situation. I bring up the example of the dented car and ask the student, "When you're older, what's something good that you could think of after you just put a big dent in your car?" We

121

brainstorm and come up with things like, "At least I can still drive the car", "At least I have insurance so that it can get fixed", or "At least I didn't get hurt."

Sometimes a lemon is so big, like a death in the family, that it's very difficult for the student to see what possibly could be good about this really bad situation.

In the case of a death, depending upon the age of the student, how the student is doing and the exact situation, I may try to help the student think of the "sugar" that might be able to be found in such a horrible situation. Together we've come up with things like:

- their relative is no longer sick or in pain

- their relative is in a better place

- they have good memories that no one can take away

- the person who passed away would want them to be sad about their passing, but they would not want their grief to prevent them from having a good life

- the person who passed away would want them to make them proud by doing their best in school and by doing whatever they can to be helpful at home

Lemon story #1: My dad had several extra-large lemons in his life as a child. His mother died when he was two-years old - so he never had a chance to develop any memories with her. Finances were really tight, so his dad decided to put his sister up for adoption in order to cut expenses. (It was much easier back then than it is now to ask someone to adopt your child.) So, all of sudden, he didn't have a sister.

Soon after this his dad decided to marry a lady who didn't really like children. In fact, one day my dad overheard his new stepmother suggesting to his dad that they put both his brother and him up for adoption, too. After hearing this, he decided to be respectful to his stepmother even when she was disrespectful to him, to focus on doing his best in school, and to stay away from her as much as possible. He didn't realize it at the time, but he had started the process of turning his lemons into lemonade.

Unfortunately, his dad's marriage turned out to be an unhappy one. His dad and stepmother argued a lot. The yelling got so bad during high school that my dad had to move out and live in a rooming house for a few weeks until things settled down.

He saw how hard his dad worked in the factory and that he didn't make much money. His dad didn't go to any school or college after high school. My dad decided that he was going to find a way to be the first person in his family to go to college.

When he asked his dad if he could help him pay for college, his dad said something like, "No, but good luck!"

So, my dad decided to go to college and work full-time at the same time in order to pay for college. It was a real grind - going to class, going to work, studying, and sleeping.

One day at college he met a lady waiting in the cafeteria line (this lady would one day become my mother). Soon after they started dating, he was so weary with the grind that he told her that he was considering dropping out of college and starting to work in the factory with his dad. He was about to give up on his goal of becoming a college graduate because it was just too much. When she heard this, she told him that if he dropped out of college that she wasn't going to date him anymore. Thankfully he changed his mind and he eventually graduated from college with honors.

But his story of turning his lemons into lemonade doesn't end there.

My dad married a strong woman. He was able to get a good job right out of college because of his hard work as a college student.

Over the years he was promoted to better and better jobs with more and more responsibility. Unfortunately, most of these jobs were very stressful (more lemons) and by the end of every day at work he was in a bad mood. I didn't know about how stressful and unpleasant his job was until I made the mistake as a teenager of asking him after work, "Did you have a good day?" He looked me straight in the eye and said, "Son, the next good day I have at work will be my first good day." I never asked him that question again.

But, because of his unhappy home life as a child, he was determined that he would have a happy home life as an adult. He used the 30 minutes that he drove home from work to change his mood from bad to good (or at least to prepare himself to fake being in a good mood). So, every day when he came home, he was in a good mood.

Looking back at this now, I don't know how he did it - but I know for sure that it definitely helped my mother, brother, and I to have a happier home life.

There's another thing that my dad did to turn his lemons into lemonade. He didn't hold it against his stepmother for the way that she treated him growing up. We drove over two hours each way a few times a year to visit my grandpa and my step-grandmother. My step-grandmother never said an unkind word to me, and she prepared delicious meals and desserts for us every time we went. Her puffy sugar cookies were so good that they melted in your mouth. I had no idea that there had ever been any problems between my dad and his stepmother until he told me about it when I was a teenager. He was a great example to me of how to respect someone who has been disrespectful to you in the past.

One more great thing about my dad - while he taught me to treat everyone with respect, he made it a point to tell me to be sure to treat people of color with an even higher level of respect because they've been treated so poorly by others in the past.

The reason that I told you about my dad's life was to honor him and to encourage you to work on turning the lemons that you have in your life into lemonade. At times you might need help from your school counselor or a professional counselor to help you do that. Some people think that asking for help is a sign of weakness - but it's actually a sign of strength to get help when you need it. Professional counseling is often available for little or no fee through health insurance. Almost everyone needs counseling at some point in their lives. Remember, I did.

Lemon story #2: I was blessed as a child because our family took long family vacations pretty much every summer. We drove to every state except Alabama, Arkansas, Louisiana, Mississippi, Hawaii, and Alaska - pulling our small camping trailer on most of the trips.

One summer we went out to the Southwest and on that trip, we visited the Six Flags Over Texas® amusement park in Arlington, Texas. One of the great rides there is the "Runaway Mine Train." It's a roller coaster with roller coaster cars that look like mine cars. The ride is supposed to simulate a mine train that is out of control. It has lots of quick drops, twists, and tight speedy turns.

My first lemon on this ride started at the very beginning. My brother and I were sitting in the front part of a mine car and my parents were sitting in the back. My mom dropped the map of the park on the floor of our mine car and she asked me to pick it up. As I reached down underneath my seat to get it, the lap bar that's designed to hold riders in place dropped down on my neck and pinned my head between my legs. As the mine car started to move, I let out a blood curdling scream, "Aaaah!!!" and the train stopped. The staff released the security bar, checked to see if I was OK, and then finally off we went.*

The ride was exciting. Near the end of it, the mine train went up a small hill and then slowed down as it entered an old mine building. Inside the building was a really neat old-fashioned saloon complete with a guy playing a piano and waitresses dressed up in western garb. They even waved to us.

It was all just a setup for the rest of the ride. They wanted us to think that the ride was pretty much over and that we could relax. All I remember next is that suddenly the mine train plunged into a completely dark hole. Everyone was screaming. At the bottom of the dark hole the track went quickly to the right and then to the left and I was thrown first against my brother and then against the side of the mine car.

Quickly we were out in the sunlight with nothing but sky above us. As I looked back, I amazingly saw that the roller coaster track somehow came up out of a man-made lake. (If you want to find out how Six Flags Over Texas® made it look like this, please go to the Respect Club blog which can be accessed through the respectclub.org website.)

My second lemon on the ride was the bruises on my legs - bruises that I got from being thrown left and right at the bottom of the dark hole. I didn't care, I just wanted to go on the ride again. In fact, we ended up going on it seven times without having to wait. My brother and I especially enjoyed hearing the surprised screams of people who had never ridden on it before as we dropped into the dark hole.

*I tell people as a joke that because of my almost getting really hurt on this ride, amusement parks around the world started having their staff check the lap bar of each car and give the "thumbs up" signal before the "all clear" signal is given for a roller coaster train to depart.

Lemon story #3: As I drove to Northwest Middle School on a Monday, it was raining cats and dogs (not literally). As I was about to park on a side street near the school, I saw a sign that read, "Street Sweeping this side Monday and Wednesday." I thought about parking there anyway because I didn't think that any street sweeping was going to be done in all that rain. Then I remembered that I have always asked my students to make good choices - so I moved my car to the other side of the street where street sweeping was done on Tuesday and Thursday. When I got out of the car to see if I was close enough to the curb and that there wasn't a fire hydrant anywhere nearby, I noticed that my car was about two feet into the yellow curb. The yellow curb means "no parking", so I backed up the car a few feet, locked it up, and went to work.

It was about 4:30 when I finished my afterschool paperwork and when I went out to my car I was shocked to see - a ticket on my windshield? How could that be? - and it was not just a minor ticket - it was a $75 ticket for parking in a handicapped zone. I looked around and I didn't see any sign that said it was a handicapped zone. Then I saw it, a blue curb. Up until that day I don't think that I'd ever seen a blue curb. When I called the parking authority, they told me that the blue curb means "handicapped parking only."

I was unhappy that I had tried to do the right thing twice, but I still ended up with a ticket. I wrote a long letter explaining what had happened to the parking authority, but they still cashed my check. In fact, a few months later they put up a really nice sign showing it was a handicapped only zone (I think that possibly they used my money to pay for it to be put up.).

So how did I turn that parking ticket into lemonade? I've used that ticket hundreds of times over the years to help students who have some type of lemon in their life. I pull it out of my desk as I tell the story in order to encourage students to make lemonade out of their lemon whatever it is (having the lemon of having to pay a $75 fine turned out to be a good thing because I made lemonade out of it - I turned a bad situation into something good).

Lemon story #4: One day, without any warning, I had more small lemons in one day than I've ever had. Here's the back story: When I worked for the YMCA®, I lived year-round at Camp Shand (a summer sleepaway camp) and paid a small amount of rent so that I could save up money for a down payment on a house. From late fall through late spring, I lived in the cook's quarters which was located in the back corner of the dining hall. During the summer I lived in an 8' x 10' room in the basement of the recreation hall (which was located only about 100 feet from the dining hall) so that the cook and his wife would have a place to live during the ten weeks of summer camp.

Since I was single at that time and I didn't have to worry about being home at a particular time, I often stayed late in my office at the downtown YMCA® building working on paperwork. One Friday night I knew that a group of about two hundred people from a Korean church was renting the entire camp facility, so I decided to work until about 2 a.m.. My hope was that when I arrived at camp everyone would be asleep, and I would be able to go to bed in peace.

Boy, was I wrong. As I made the final left hand turn off the camp road into the parking lot, I saw that every light in the camp was on - even the large floodlights that illuminated the outdoor basketball court. Adults and their children were everywhere. I saw a group of adults standing near what we called Penryn Lake (even though it's just a large pond). Some were fishing, others were using the fire ring near the lake to fry up fish that had just been caught. To my knowledge no one had ever cooked and ate fish from the lake before.

I was surprised by how quiet it was even though all those people were milling around - so I decided to try to go to sleep. As I was just about asleep, I was jolted awake by loud singing in Korean.

I walked up to the top floor of the recreation hall to find out what was going on. I saw that all of the wooden benches from our outdoor chapel had been set up in rows and in the front of the room about twenty men in choir robes were singing hymns.

I knew that that there was no way that I was going to be able to sleep in the recreation hall, so I decided to take my sleeping bag and pillow and walk over to sleep in the cook's quarters.

After laying down, almost immediately I heard children singing. It was coming from the dining hall, so I decided to walk outside and close the wooden shutters to reduce the noise. It was now about 3 a.m. and as I was closing a shutter, I peeked in and saw an adult talking to a young child and I heard her say, "You're not tired, are you?"

Suddenly, my left foot was underwater. I said to myself, "How could that be? - I'm more than 30 feet from the creek that feeds the lake."

As I looked down at my feet, I saw a large empty can of tuna (about 9 inches in diameter) that had been left over from summer camp. The can had filled up with water from rain after camp ended. I had accidentally stepped on the left-hand edge of the can with my right foot, the can flipped over, and the water spilled all over my left foot.

I wasn't happy because now I was going to have to take another shower in order to get ready for bed. I think that I thought to myself, "Wow, what else could go wrong?"

After the shower, while I was sitting on the bed drying off my legs, I felt something that I felt about twenty years earlier when I had a dog, and I instantly knew what it was - fleas were biting me! (I found out later that the cook's dog had fleas that summer and had infested the entire cook's quarters).

I had to get out of there, so I got dressed quickly, picked up my sleeping bag and pillow, and started to walk back to the recreation hall.

As I got about halfway there, suddenly every light in the whole camp went out - a complete power failure. I remember looking up and seeing the only light I had - the moon.

The moonlight allowed me to walk up a small hill to the trailer where the camp facility manager lived. I pounded on the door and yelled, "Dave, please call the power company - the power has failed!" I woke him up from a sound sleep and of course, when he tried to turn on the lights, nothing happened. He came to the door using his flashlight, and he said, sounding startled and groggy, "I'll call them."

As I walked back toward the recreation hall, I saw that the doors at the top of the steps were open, and an eerie glow of light was coming through. I wondered what the light was.

Much to my surprise, when I walked through the doors, I saw each member of the choir, still in their choir robes, lying lengthwise on a chapel bench trying to sleep with their hands folded across their body. The glow I'd seen was from the dim emergency lighting that had come on when the power failed. It was a surreal experience - something like you'd see in a movie.

The emergency lighting allowed me to see when I walked downstairs to my room in the basement. I settled in, thinking that finally my problems (lemons) were over for the night.

But no - soon after putting my head on the pillow I heard the gurgling sounds of water and the hissing sound of air under pressure being released. I wondered what it was - and then it hit me. Someone had flushed a toilet in the recreation hall and the water system that pumped water from the well was trying to refill the toilet. But that wasn't going to happen - because there was no electric power to the pump because of the power failure!

So, I had to go to each bathroom in the entire camp, be sure that everyone was out of the bathroom, lock each door so that no one else could go in, and put up a handwritten sign that read, "Bathroom closed - please use the extra portable toilets in the parking lot. Thank you!"

I think that it was about 4 a.m. before I was finally able to get to sleep.

The reason that I shared this story is that I wanted to let you know that you most likely will have days in your life just like this - days that are filled with lemons, days when many things go wrong. When you're having one of these days, my suggestion is that you do what I tried to do, just roll with whatever comes your way and do your best to make lemonade out of your lemons.

(After I wrote this, I decided to send it into our local newspaper for their "I know a story" column. I suggested that the title of the story be, "Nightmare at Camp Shand.")

(Please don't think for a minute that my life has been pretty much lemon free other than the lemons in the stories that I've shared so far. My first wife of 10 years told me that I was a "nice guy", but then divorced me because she wanted to do her own thing. I married a strong woman the second time around and last year we celebrated our 30th wedding anniversary. Over 40 years ago, I had a "grand mal" epileptic seizure out of the blue - thankfully other people were with me when it happened - and I've been on medication since then to control it. I was laid off from three jobs - even though I was doing a good job and I was giving my best effort. A few years ago, without any warning, I developed multiple blood clots in my right leg, and I could have died if one of the clots had broken loose and gone to my lungs. So now I must wear an ugly knee-high compression sock and take medication for the rest of my life to help prevent more clots. Over the years I've tried to remember my "sugar" and to use it to turn my lemons into lemonade. You can too!)

I have given many students a sticker that has a picture of a lemon and a picture of a glass of lemonade along with the words: *"When life hands you a lemon (a problem), make lemonade, in other words make the best of a bad situation and become stronger!"*

13

SELFISHNESS DAMAGES RELATIONSHIPS

*Contrary to what many people think, a good life
isn't found by constantly seeking personal gain
and personal pleasure (selfishness) - it's found in
caring about, loving, and serving others.*

As a teen and a young adult, I never heard anyone talk about the
two main values in our society. If they did, I wasn't paying
attention.

I'm not sure where, but I heard or read somewhere that the two
main values in our society are personal gain and personal
pleasure. Think about it, aren't they the main two things that
most people are concerned about? People want to get as much as
they can (money, stuff, etc.) and they want as much fun as
possible. Unfortunately, many people have been brainwashed by
the media and by their "friends" into thinking that personal gain
and personal pleasure - in other words selfishness - is the way to
happiness. Too many people think that if something's exciting or
feels good, just do it.

We're naturally selfish - we're concerned about having food we
like, good clothes, a nice place to live, all kinds of stuff, and lots
of fun. Face it, we live in a "Me First" society - many people want
what they want when they want it. However, too much
selfishness can be destructive to yourself and to your
relationships with others. It may not seem to make any sense,
but forgetting about yourself and focusing on caring about,
loving, and serving others is a good way to find happiness.

Here's a quick example of what I'm trying to communicate: Before my wife and I had children we went to amusement parks and rode all of the fast thrill rides from opening to closing. After we had children, my main source of joy was no longer from the excitement of riding the rides that I wanted to ride (selfishness). Instead, it was from seeing the joy on my children's faces as they had fun riding the rides that they wanted to ride. My focus was off of myself. My joy came from loving them by going on their favorite rides (and at 6'6" tall I didn't fit very well into the little train that they wanted me to ride on with them). It may be hard to believe, but I got just as much enjoyment sitting in the shade watching them go around in circles on the little kiddie airplanes as I did when I was going on the fastest scariest thrill ride.

If you decide to get married someday in the future, it's very important to realize that a big problem that you're going to have to battle on a daily basis is selfishness. You go through most of your single life with yourself as your #1 concern. If you get married, all of a sudden after a few words said by a person who has a license to perform marriages, someone else that you love is supposed to be your #1 concern. You're now #2. (If you have children, you become an even lower priority.) When you get married - you make a promise to love, honor, and cherish your lifelong mate regardless of whether you feel like doing it.

To many people who get married, having to put someone else first is a big shock - it means that they can no longer say or do whatever they want whenever they want. It takes a while for some people to adjust to this new reality because old habits are often slow to die. I have to confess that there are times when I'm not happy about having to put my wife first and sometimes I fail to put her first. I have to try each day to be less selfish and to do a better job of loving my wife and family.

I realize that it's hard for some people to understand that being selfish will not help them to have a good life. Let me explain it in another way - too much selfishness is like eating too much candy. If you keep eating too much candy, you'll eventually end up overweight or sick. Too much selfishness gradually damages your relationships with others. Quite frankly, they get sick of your selfishness.

An idea for families:

A few students and I came up with a somewhat silly but fun way to help people in families discourage selfishness - when someone says something that's just out and out selfish, for example bragging about how great they are or demanding what they want - the other people in the family together say "goy!" in a funny way. Goy! stands for "**g**et **o**ff **y**ourself." Usually everyone starts laughing after it's said. Talk this idea over with your family and see if they want to try it. (I've seen strong friends use this idea to successfully help each other be less selfish.)

"A selfish person may be happy for a short period of time, but I've never met a selfish person who's been happy, content, and fulfilled throughout their entire life."

"Selfishness is like a drought to the beautiful flower of a healthy friendship - it eventually makes it wither."

"Selfishness is the greatest curse of the human race."
- William E. Gladstone

It's true that talking about ourselves a lot (a form of selfishness) helps us to feel good about ourselves. But the problem is that if you pretty much only talk about yourself, people usually get tired of that quickly. Instead of talking about yourself most of the time, focus on getting other people to talk about themselves by asking them an open-ended question (one that can't be answered by simply saying "yes" or "no" - maybe something like, "So, what do you like to do in your spare time?"). Listen, share some things related to what they said, share what you like to do in your spare time, and then ask another open-ended question.

Have you noticed that people who have the selfish, 'I'm going to do whatever feels good whenever I feel like doing it' attitude, almost always eventually mess up their lives?

14

AN UNCONTROLLED TONGUE ISN'T A GOOD THING

It's very hard for many people to get their tongue under control by thinking before talking

I messed up yesterday. I talked to my wife in a way that wasn't kind. Instead of treating her like an adult and expressing my negative thoughts and feelings in a calm constructive manner about a particular situation, I talked to her like she was the child, and I was the parent - not a good way to treat her with respect and to make her feel loved. Thankfully, we were able to talk it out and I told her that I was sorry for expressing my thoughts and feelings in a negative destructive way. She forgave me.

The reason I brought this up is to give you an example that, even after all these years of marriage, I'm still making bad choices using my tongue. Unfortunately, it's a daily battle that sometimes the tongue wins.

When my son was in his teens, he seemed to think that he should say what's on his mind when it's on his mind. He thought that holding things in wasn't good for him - you know, like he might develop stomach problems. We tried to explain to him that sometimes things need to be left unsaid or at the very least not be said until everyone has had a chance to cool off and a calm constructive conversation can take place. We've tried to teach our children to ask themselves questions in their minds before saying something. Questions like: 1. Am I calm? 2. Is the other person calm? 3. Does it need to be said? 4. Will saying it make the situation better? 5. Is it a good choice to say it? 6. How can I say what needs to be said in a way that's as positive as possible? 7. Is this the right time and place to say it?

I realize that the importance of controlling your tongue has already been discussed on pp. 92-94. I decided to include more detailed information in this chapter of the book because I think that it's important to emphasize the fact that many people don't realize how important it is to use their tongue wisely and how much damage an uncontrolled tongue can cause to your relationships with other people.

You may be forgiven after you say something without thinking, but sometimes it takes a long time for the damage to be repaired. (This is because people have a tendency to remember what you said thoughtlessly and replay it in their minds. Their trust that you will not try to hurt them with your words has been broken - and unfortunately trust often takes a long while to be rebuilt.)

I encourage you to practice controlling your tongue along with me by thinking before talking. I know that it's not easy. Learning how to use your words in a positive manner will help you to build healthy relationships in all areas of your life.

15

HOW TO WORK OUT CONFLICTS IN A POSITIVE PEACEFUL WAY

Knowing how to work out conflicts in a positive peaceful way is a skill that you're going to need throughout life

No matter how hard you try to avoid them, you're still going to have conflicts at times throughout your life (A good number of my students tell me, "I have some type of conflict with somebody almost every day.") It's important that you prepare yourself in advance to try to avoid them when possible and to work them out in a positive peaceful manner when they do happen. Here's some information about conflicts using a question-and-answer format:

Q. What is a conflict?

A. A conflict is a serious disagreement over something. A conflict often occurs when the wants and needs of one person are not the same as the wants and needs of another person. (For example, when a person wants to be treated with respect and the other person refuses to treat them with respect.)

Q. What are some of the things that conflicts start over?

A.
- Disrespectful things that others say and do
- Disrespectful things that others say behind your back
- Getting into someone else's business
- Untrue rumors, gossip
- Who's right and who's wrong
- Bragging about something

- Not keeping a secret (that's not safety-related) of a friend
- Friendships
- Relationships
- Feeling left out
- Wanting to "fit in"
- Selfishness
- Wanting something that someone else has
- Cheating in a game
- Putting hands on someone else
- Touching or damaging the property of someone else
- Stealing someone else's stuff
- Negative social media posts
- . . . and many more

Q. Why do some students seem to enjoy starting a conflict?

A.
- They like the excitement of starting conflicts or being involved in conflicts (many of these students mistakenly think that doing their best in school isn't that important)

- Some students like using conflicts to put others down so that they can feel better about themselves

- Some people have never learned that conflicts sometimes lead to violence and that violence is a horrible thing

Q. How does a student minimize the number of conflicts that they have in their life?

A.
- Learn to have self-control of the tongue (failing to control your tongue causes more conflicts that anything else)

- Learn to have self-control of anger (combining a conflict with anger can lead to violence)

Q. How do you work out a conflict in a positive peaceful way? (Acronym: CONFLICTS)

A.
- **C**alm yourself by taking deep breaths - in through your nose and slowly out through your mouth and by trying to think as positive as possible (it's very difficult to work out a conflict if one or both people are feeling angry)

- Be **o**pen to working out the conflict in a positive peaceful way (in other words, be ready and willing to do so)

- **N**ever use violence (it only makes things worse and someone could get really hurt)

- Be willing to **f**orgive because forgiving helps you to drain your anger barrel - and that makes you less likely to lose your self-control and explode

- Really **l**isten when the other person speaks and maybe even say in your own words what you think they said

- **I**dentify what's causing the conflict. Use I-messages to tell the other person how you feel in a kind way (I feel _____ when you _____.)

- Be ready to **c**ompromise - remember that no one gets their own way all of the time

- Use your words to calmly **t**alk about possible positive solutions (ways to make things better) to the conflict - for example: sharing something, playing together, taking turns, apologizing (it's great when I hear one of my elementary school students say something like, "Let's say sorry, let it go, and start playing again").

- Agree on the best **s**olution. (If that one doesn't work, try another one that you agree upon.)

I hope that remembering the acronym CONFLICTS will help you to work out conflicts throughout your life.

"It takes at least two people to have an argument - don't be one of them."

"Have you noticed how easily people are offended (make themselves angry quickly) these days - it's almost like they're looking for things to be offended by. If only people could learn to have really thick armor - so thick that all verbal arrows from other people would just bounce off - boing!"

16

THE IMPORTANCE OF GOOD COMMUNICATION SKILLS

Developing these skills will help you throughout your life

Unfortunately, the communication skills of many people in our society are not good. Proof of this fact are all of the arguments, misunderstandings, and conflicts that people have, not to mention how many times people jump to negative conclusions without having all the facts.

Communication can have many goals including;

- trying to get other people to understand how you really feel

- trying to find out what another other person is really like

- teaching and/or learning

- trying to solve problems and/or work out conflicts

- trying in a positive way to get a person to change their behavior for the better

- entertainment

Let's break down face-to-face communication in more depth. It's a lot more complicated than people realize.

When two people are trying to communicate, they're both senders and receivers at the same time. What? Here's how: When person #1 talks, they're being a sender (sending a message) through their words, tone of voice, and their body language (the expression on their face, whether their arms are at their sides or crossed in front of them, etc.) At the same time as they're talking, they're receiving (taking in a message) in the form of non-verbal feedback (a smile, a frown, sighing, getting red in the face from anger, body language, sucking their teeth, shaking their head "no", nodding "yes", leaning forward, rolling their eyes etc.) that's being sent from person #2.

Communication continues as person #2 starts to speak and the roles are reversed. The roles reverse each time a person starts talking.

So how does an attempt to communicate turn into bad communication? Bad communication has many causes such as:

- the sender not choosing the right time and place for the communication to take place

- the sender trying to communicate right away instead of waiting until both they and the receiver have calmed themselves down and are ready for good constructive communication

- the sender not being a good sender by saying things in a disrespectful tone, saying things in a disrespectful way (like yelling), by using phrases like "You always" or "You never", not thinking about what they're going to say before they say it, saying things in a negative and/or accusing tone of voice, and/or saying things with a grumpy look on their face and/or saying things with their arms crossed (negative body language).

- the receiver not listening well - possibly by not paying attention (maybe even trying to do something at the same time like watching TV, playing a game, or texting), by not really focusing on what the sender is trying to communicate, by not really caring about what the sender is saying, by jumping to a negative conclusion even before the sender has finished speaking, by

144

being quickly offended, etc. Learning to really listen, especially to the emotions that are sometimes hidden behind the words, is very difficult for some people.

So, how do you become a better face-to-face communicator? The only way to do it is to practice. Practice trying to communicate when the time and place is as good as possible, practice choosing your words carefully by thinking before talking (please don't shoot arrows at others by being disrespectful with your words), and practice trying to say what you need to say in as positive a way as possible. (When you have the right words and you have the right tone in your voice, it's more likely that the receiver will be able to stay focused on what you're trying to communicate.)

Be aware of your feelings and make sure that you're calm enough to have good constructive communication with someone before starting to have a conversation. If you don't, you're more likely to say something that you shouldn't say.

Notice the feedback that you're getting from the receiver and try to make positive adjustments to what you're saying or even postpone the conversation if necessary (if you feel a need to postpone due to making yourself angry or the other person making themselves angry during the conversation, possibly say something like, "I'm feeling like this isn't a good time to have this conversation - would it be OK if we talk about this later today or sometime tomorrow after we have a good night's sleep?")

Practice trying to make sure that the words you're saying match your body language. If you're trying to be as positive as possible with your words but have a grumpy expression on your face and/or your arms are crossed, this is sending a confusing message to the receiver which could lead to a misunderstanding.

When you're sitting down and listening, lean forward and look the sender in the eye (unless it's culturally disrespectful for you to do so) with a neutral (neither positive nor negative) expression on your face. This shows the sender that you're trying to listen. Turn off anything that could be distracting.

Do whatever you can to stay out of an argument (a conversation where both people are shooting arrows back and forth at each other). Arguments damage relationships instead of making them better.

Some people find it helpful to keep a journal as they try to improve their communication skills. They write down what they said that was good (positive) constructive communication and what was bad (negative) destructive communication. They think about what they could have said differently so that maybe the next time the communication will have a better outcome.

More than likely you're going to have people in your life who really aren't interested in having good communication with you. For your sake, please handle these pains in a positive way using the suggestions on pp. 55-57. Good luck as you practice improving your communication skills!

(I read somewhere that we tend to stop listening to the other person in the conversation about fifteen seconds before we say something back - that's because our mind is developing what we're going to say, and we can't do two things well at the same time. With practice, we can learn to wait until the other person is done talking and then possibly even paraphrase what they just said - for example, "So, what I hear you saying is that . . ." to make sure that you've heard correctly and to be able to adjust what you were about to say if necessary.)

Communication story #1: When an after-school meeting ended at our school last year, two teachers started sharing stories about their grown daughters. I usually leave these meetings right away so that I can get back to working on my afterschool

146

counselor paperwork. On this day, I hung around for about ten minutes to hear the stories because they were really humorous. I just listened. I didn't say a word. When I eventually left, I said to both of them, "Thanks for the entertainment!" They laughed - and of course, I didn't share their stories with anyone else.

Communication story #2: I was not a good sender a few months ago when I said to my son, "You always leave a blob of toothpaste on the sink." The most important thing he heard was the word "always" and his response was, "I don't always do that."

He was right. Instead of accusing him of "always" doing something or giving him a command like, "Don't leave a toothpaste blob on the sink anymore!", I should have given him a positive request like, "Would you please do me a favor and be more careful to not leave a blob of toothpaste on the sink? - I've had to clean it up a few times." Please keep in mind that people are more likely to respond in a positive way to requests than commands.

Communication story #3: I hear about students jumping to negative conclusions on a regular basis at my school. For example, if a student is sitting at table "A" in the cafeteria and two other students are at table "B" talking, laughing, and periodically looking over at the student at table "A" - the student at table "A" often jumps to the negative conclusion that the students at table "B" are saying bad things about them behind their back and are laughing at them. For some reason jumping to negative conclusions is a habit that many people seem to have (including me at times).

When a student comes to my office expressing their anger about "someone talking about me", I listen and then suggest that they use "My Shield" as described on pp. 40-43 in this type of situation. Stop, breathe, think positive things like "Maybe they're not talking about me", "I can't control if they're talking about me", "I'm not going to make myself angry and let them have power over me.", "This isn't worth getting angry about", "I'm not concerned about whether or not they're talking about me", "I'm still a good person even if they're talking about me.", "Maybe I need to talk to the school counselor about this because it seems like they may need help", etc.). I also suggest to the student that if they're in a similar situation in the future, that they completely ignore the students at table "B". And finally, I strongly suggest that if it happens again, they don't go up to the people at table "B" and say, "Are you two talking about me?" The reason for this suggestion is that very few people tell the truth when they're asked this question - and conflicts often start after this question is asked. (I hold a mediation for the students involved if necessary.)

Positive words
Positive tone of voice
+   Positive body language
Good Communication

Good communicators realize that how they say something (especially the tone and the volume of their voice) is more important for good communication than the words they say.

If possible, especially with family members, try not to let the sun go down while still feeling angry. If you're both not too tired, try to have a positive constructive conversation about the problem and try to make things better. Apologize if necessary, and be willing to forgive the other person. ("Can you forgive me?", is a beautiful question to ask.)

16

PEERS HAVE TOO MUCH POWER

Watch out for the negative power of peers

So, who do you think has the biggest influence on the behavior of people? You guessed it - peers. Many people are influenced by their peers (people their own age) to make bad choices of behavior in order to fit in. These bad (disrespectful) choices sometimes have long term negative consequences.

Let's try to understand why peers have more influence and are more important to many people than anyone else. Could it be that we see and talk to peers every day? Could it be that we put more effort into developing our relationships with peers compared to anyone else? Could it be that peers give us positive and negative feedback about what we say and do every day? Could it be that peers are so powerful because we think that we need their approval and acceptance in order to feel good about ourselves and we tremendously fear their rejection? Could all of these things be reasons that many people have a closer relationship with their peers than anyone else?

Speaking of rejection from peers, I really understand why so many people fear it and desperately want to fit in because I used to feel the same way. Here's one example from my life: I ended up going to a new high school for my senior year because we moved. I didn't know anyone, they didn't know me, and my #1 concern was whether or not my peers would like me. I was so paranoid and so concerned about peers not liking me that I hardly said a word to anyone during the first two months of the school year. I was afraid that if I opened my mouth people wouldn't like me. Thankfully as the year went along, I started to talk more, and I made a few strong friends.

What I didn't realize at the time was that I was allowing my peers to control my life. Are you or any of your peers making the same bad choice? I had become a people pleaser - a person who tries to please others to get their approval. A key turning point in the life of a person is when they decide to try to make a good choice in every situation regardless of what others say, do, or think. A word of caution: After you make this decision to try to make a good choice in every situation, don't expect an overnight change in regard to being concerned about whether or not your peers like you. It takes time to gradually become a stronger and stronger person. You'll know that you're making progress when you notice you're not so concerned about pleasing your peers as you used to be - especially disrespectful peers who regularly make bad choices.

Over time with practice, you'll reach the point where you'll be in the habit of trying to make a good choice in every situation. Here's a suggestion for handling peer rejection: If a peer puts you down after you make what you thought was a good choice in a particular situation, try not to get yourself too worked up about it because that peer probably isn't a strong friend anyway. Instead, do your best to ignore what the disrespectful peer had to say or have a private calm conversation with them about the situation if you think that you can talk about it in a constructive manner (or ask your school counselor to mediate the situation if you think that would help). If that doesn't work, focus on putting in the effort to make more strong friends by being a strong friend (strong friendship was discussed on pp. 28-29).

"You're in charge of using the five tools to build a good life. No one else can do it for you. Things so far in your life may not have gone well, maybe through no fault of your own and/or you may have made some bad choices but remember that "what's over is over" - and you can still use the tools to build a good life. It's never too late!

If you've made bad choices, admit them and apologize. (Unfortunately, you can't control whether or not people will forgive you.) Next, try to make up for what you've done if you can. Finally, learn from your bad choices, forgive yourself, and move forward toward achieving your goals in life.

You can make it much more likely that you'll have a good life by trying to live your life as a strong person every day. Take time to prepare yourself mentally to be strong before you start the day (put your armor on). Remember that you're a good person and that feeling good about yourself doesn't depend upon what others say, do, or think. If people don't like you because you're trying to live your life as a strong person, that's their choice. It's out of your control.

Find a group of strong friends who can help you to become and stay strong. It's true that this group is sometimes hard to find, but you can find strong friends by being a strong friend!"

151

"A strong person has discipline - they try to do the most important thing instead of just doing what they feel like doing."

"A strong person is thankful for all the blessings that they have compared to so many other people in the world. They don't take what they have, even if it's not much, for granted."

NOTES:

SECTION 5: TRUE STORIES - FOR AGES 15 & UP

The following true stories were not included in the main part of the book because they are not appropriate for elementary school as well as possibly intermediate and middle school students. I included them in the book because I think that they may be helpful to older students.

Choices story: Sadly I've met a good number of people who've messed up their lives by make the choice to use alcohol and/or other drugs. Many of us don't think of alcohol as a drug because the media and our popular culture has glamorized how "fun" it is to use. However, it changes how the brain works just like other drugs. Because of their size, women are more likely to develop heart disease, cancer, and liver disease from drinking than men. Almost 1 out of every 5 teens who drink has a serious drinking problem. The earlier a person starts drinking, the more likely they'll become an alcoholic. About 1 out of every 10 adults who drink becomes an alcoholic. Binge drinking, more than 4 drinks for adult women and 5 drinks for adult men in one sitting, is increasing. Alcohol is the most abused drug in the world. As you read this depressing information, please don't think that everyone is drinking - 30 out of every 100 adults don't drink at all and many adults only drink in moderation (not to get drunk). Please be strong and choose not to follow the crowd of people who drink too much. You don't need it to have fun.

Forgiving story: I also have struggled at times to forgive others as an adult. I ran a Community Center (a workout facility similar to a YMCA®) for seven years and built up the membership from 150 to over 1,100 members. The Board of Directors (a group of volunteers from the community who supervised me) wanted to sell the existing building and move to a bigger building that was located on the main road. I carefully made up a budget for the bigger building which clearly showed that we could not afford to move to the bigger building. I told them that the Community Center would eventually go out of business if they moved. They didn't listen to me, and they decided to go through with the move.

About a year after the move, I resigned my position and ten months later I went back to school full-time to become qualified to be a school counselor while I worked part-time to pay the bills. Every day during those ten months while I was selling appliances, I thought negative thoughts about the Board members, and I made myself angry. I could feel the anger in the pit of my stomach. I asked myself over and over again in my head, "How could they make such a poor decision and flush seven years of my hard work (as well as the work of other dedicated staff members) to grow the membership down the toilet?" I was torturing myself by feeling angry every day. During all this time the Board members were not feeling bad about their decision because they still thought it was a good one. Finally, with the help of a counselor, I was able to forgive them and not let their bad choice do any more damage to my life (sadly the Community Center did eventually go out of business).

Friendly story #1 (Caution - graphic): Being a "people pleaser" (going along with what other people want you to do to make them happy or to avoid being rejected) or giving in to negative peer pressure can have serious consequences. The 13-year-old son of someone I once worked with was encouraged by his "friends" to do something that they said would make him feel really good for a few minutes and wasn't dangerous. He made the bad choice to go along with what they wanted him to do. Sadly, he died when his heart stopped after about a minute. His parents have had a giant painful hole in their hearts for over 25 years - a hole that opens up every year on his birthday when they remember how old he would have been. All of this pain could have been avoided if he had just been strong and told his "friends" - "I'm not doing that" and then walked away. (The people who encouraged him to make this bad choice weren't strong friends, because a strong friend never encourages a friend to do anything that even has the possibility of being a bad choice. Now they have to live for the rest of their lives with the fact that they encouraged their friend to make a bad choice that ended in his death.)

Friendly story #2 (Caution - talks about illegal drug use): Years back as a substitute teacher a student told me that he and his "friends" smoked illegal marijuana together regularly, that they were really close, and that they would pretty much do "anything" for each other. I listened and then politely said that from everything I've read, smoking marijuana is even more dangerous than smoking cigarettes because it's been shown to cause cancer and it can change how well the brain works. He said that all that stuff about the dangers of marijuana was made up by the government. A few weeks later the leader of the group was busted for marijuana distribution and the group of "friends", who would do "anything" for each other, scattered to the wind and no longer did anything together. They weren't strong friends.

Handling pains in a positive way story #1: While I was still working at the Community Center, I had to fire someone from their job because they were constantly late. It was really important for her to be on time because her job was to supervise a large room with all kinds of exercise and weightlifting equipment - and that room had to be supervised at all times in case a member had some type of emergency.

After two verbal warnings and one written warning, I fired her in a polite respectful manner by calming saying, "Unfortunately you're late again, remember you signed a form saying that you understand you'll be fired the next time you're late. I'm sorry." It was not an easy thing to do, but it had to be done.

Much to my surprise, about six months later after I'd resigned from the Community Center, she became my boss at my job selling appliances part-time and thankfully she treated me well. She never told anyone that she had worked for me and that I had fired her. She didn't hold anything against me - possibly because of the way that I treated her when I fired her.

Handling pains in a positive way story #2 (Caution - graphic): A 16-year-old high school student, who lived two towns over from ours, decided to take a boombox to the town park to listen to music with curse words in it. Soon a 24-year-old man, who was with his 6-year-old son, came up to him and asked him to turn the music down or turn it off because he didn't want his son hearing those words. An argument started and the 24-year-old ended up punching the teen multiple times in the head. The teen was rushed to the hospital, but sadly died a few days later. So, one person died, one person will be in jail for many years, and a young boy will grow up without his father.

Handling pains in a positive way story #3 (Caution - graphic): A college student was walking in a small college town talking on his cell phone close to midnight and a drunk guy came up to him and said in a loud rude tone, "Who are you talking to?" The college student said in a smart way back, "Well, not you!" Unfortunately, those were the last words he spoke - he was beaten to death by the drunk guy and the drunk guy's friend.

A common thread runs through the last two horrible stories. I could be wrong, but it seems like neither of the people who died knew how to handle pains in a positive way. If they would've learned at a young age never to say anything negative or smart to someone who's potentially violent or to someone who they don't know, possibly these tragedies could have been prevented.

Self-control of body story #1 - I was talking with a 4th grade girl who had only been in our school for about a month after she had just been sent to the office for punching a guy in the face. I asked her why she did it. She said without any hesitation, "He called my friend a camel, what else was I supposed to do?" This gave me a great opportunity to teach her about how to use My Armor and My Shield. Thankfully she learned to control her anger better as the school year went by.

Self-control of the body #2 (Caution - graphic): I was getting a haircut one day and started talking with the hair stylist. I think she asked me what I did for a living, and I told her that I was a school counselor. During the conversation we somehow got talking about fighting in school and she shared that she still regrets what she did to another girl in high school. She said that she got into an argument with the girl, pretty much over nothing, and it ended up in a fight. She won the fight, but during it the other girl ended up hitting her head on the ground. She said that the other girl could have reported her to the police, but she didn't.

The big problem was that the brain of the other girl was injured and to this day it isn't working right, which has made it very hard for her to keep a steady job and have a good life. The hair stylist told me that sometimes she sees the girl walking by herself downtown and she makes it a point to go over and talk to her to ask how she's doing. The girl never brings up what happened and seems to have forgiven her. The hair stylist also told me that she wishes that she had been a person of peace during high school so this never would have happened. I asked her permission to include this story in this book.

Self-control of the body story #3 (Caution - graphic): Two students I worked with at the Alternative School (a school for students who were temporarily thrown out of their home school due to poor behavior) regularly had a problem getting along with other students. One of the students, Jose*, was on his way walking home when he stopped to talk to a friend on the sidewalk right in front of a house. They were talking loudly for a while and a person who was sitting on their front porch asked them to move along so that he could have some peace and quiet. Jose didn't like anyone telling him what to do and he got into a heated argument with the guy on the porch.

Jose left and walked over to Miguel's* house (another student from the Alternative School) and told him what had happened - that he was angry because he had been disrespected by the guy on the porch. They decided to walk back and confront the guy. Miguel made the really bad choice of deciding to bring his dad's gun along.

They confronted the guy on the porch and Miguel suggested that they settle the problem with a fight in the alley nearby. Shockingly, during the fight Miguel pulled out the gun and shot the guy in the abdomen. Thankfully the guy didn't die. Miguel got a sentence of five years in prison for shooting him.

*All names changed to protect the guilty

Self-control of the body story #4 (Caution - graphic): Telling this story has helped some of my students to really think about why it's so important to become a person of peace.

I start by explaining that when a part of your body is injured, your body sends extra fluid and white blood cells to the injured area to help with the healing process. "So, if I hit my index finger right now with a hammer, my finger would start to swell (get bigger) really quickly." Next, I tell them the true story:

When I was a substitute teacher in a middle school before I was able to get a school counselor position, two boys got into a fistfight in the hallway after arguing about stolen lunch dessert money. During the fight one boy fell and hit his head on the floor. As his head hit the floor, his brain bounced and slammed into the inside of his skull (I clap my hands hard once to simulate his head hitting the floor and this helps my students to really listen). He was unconscious and blood was coming out of his ear. The EMT's arrived within 5 minutes and rushed him to the hospital.

At the hospital, they immediately shaved his head while they ran tests to find out if needed to have emergency brain surgery because of swelling of his brain. When the brain is injured, it has no place to swell because it's right up against the skull. If it swells too much, he could lose his hearing. If it swells too much, he could lose his sight. If it swells too much, he could die. The boy had to have surgery to remove a part of his skull in order to relieve the pressure in his brain. Thankfully, they saved him.

He came very close to dying because neither boy was able to control their body, anger, or tongue. If this fight had happened outside of school, the boy probably would have died. So, one boy almost died and other boy was sent to the juvenile detention center and got a criminal record - all from an argument over 50 cents. I hope that they were able to forgive each other, become people of peace, and have a good life.

Self-control of their body story #5 (Caution - graphic): I once had an 8th grade student who did well in school when he worked hard but had a real problem of getting into fights outside of school - I'm talking 2 or 3 fights a week. He was trapped in the bad habit of trying to maintain his "reputation" through violence. I talked to him about it several times. He listened respectfully to me, but he didn't think that it was a big deal, and he didn't think that it was important for him to become a person of peace.

One Monday morning before school, the principal came into my office and asked me to talk to Billy (name changed to protect the guilty) because he had beaten someone up pretty badly over the weekend.

So, I looked for Billy on Monday and he wasn't there. The same thing happened on Tuesday. Now it was Wednesday, and I was starting to get worried. I asked his friends, "Do you guys know why Billy hasn't been in school? - he's almost never absent." They said, "Oh, haven't you heard?" The tone in their voice made it sound like he had died. I said, "No, I haven't heard." They said, "Well, he moved." I said, "He moved? - he never said anything about moving." They said, "Didn't you hear?" I said, "No, please tell me." They said, "After he beat up that kid on Saturday, a few of the kid's cousins came down from New York and showed up at Billy's house. Billy opened the door, and they asked him if he was the kid who beat up their cousin." They said that Billy admitted that he had and said that it should have never happened. The cousins said something like, "Well, it's not going to happen again." Billy said, "No, it's not going to happen again." The cousins said, "You don't understand, what we're saying (as they showed him their guns under their shirts in their belts) is that you and your family are going to have to move out of town."

So, he and his family packed up and left town. This is what happened to a student who tried to keep his reputation through violence.

Self-control of anger story: - One day I received a call from Mr. Berger upstairs in social studies class. He wanted to know if I had time to calm down a student who wanted to punch a girl. I said sure and the student came down to my office. He told me that he was really angry because a girl had made fun of him (disrespected him). He said that he had a cold for about a week and now the boogers in each nostril had become hard because he didn't blow his nose enough to get everything out. The girl said, "Ooh, it looks like Corn Flakes® are coming out of your nose!" He thought that comment was rude, he felt embarrassed and then angry - and he was just about to punch her. I told him that I was glad he made the good choice not to punch her. Then we talked about what he could have said to her that would be positive or funny. We came up with a few things like, "Sorry my nose is kind of nasty, I just can't seem to get rid of this cold", "I think that it looks more like Rice Krispies® than Corn Flakes®!", etc. The first statement may have helped her to have some empathy for him and the second statement may have helped them to have a good laugh together.

Self-Control of the tongue story (Caution - graphic): Over the years I've read many articles in the newspaper after something horrible has happened, like someone getting shot. Almost always the article says something like, "Witnesses say that there was an argument between the two men, before one of them pulled out a gun." Strong people have self-control of the tongue and do whatever they can to stay out of arguments.

Q. In your opinion, what are the most important things that a person should do in order to have a good life?

A. Learn and practice "The Big Three"™ every day: Be respectful, Be industrious, Be safe

(A respectful person respects their job, others, and themselves. An industrious person works hard every day trying to achieve their goals. A safe person doesn't do anything that's unsafe - even when they're having fun. In other words, they don't do anything that could possibly harm others or themselves in any way.)

TRAITS OF A BEEAUTIFUL STUDENT™*:*
(These traits are great ones for elementary school students to learn and practice.)

Bee **A**ttentive   Bee **B**rave   Bee **C**aring

Bee **D**isciplined   Bee **E**mpathetic   Bee **F**orgiving

Bee **G**rateful   Bee **H**onest   Bee **I**ndustrious

Bee **J**oyful   Bee **K**ind   Bee **L**oyal

Bee **M**odest   Bee **N**oble   Bee **O**ptimistic

Bee **P**ositive   Bee **Q**uestioning   Bee **R**espectful

Bee **S**afe   Bee **T**houghtful   Bee **U**nselfish

Bee **V**ictorious   Bee **W**ise   Bee **X**cellent

Bee **Y**ourself   Bee **Z**estful

FINAL WORD

My sincere hope is that this book has helped you to learn the five tools of a strong person and that you'll decide to use these tools to build a good life for yourself. Unfortunately, it's not easy trying to live your life as a strong person in today's disrespectful society - but let there be no doubt, if you practice using the tools every day, you can build a good life filled with joy - and that's what I'm wishing you!

(Please be sure to check out the Epilogue on p. 165 about the cultural revolution that we need in order to increase the level of respect in our society. An index of true stories, a list of recommended books, information about Respect Club™, information about the author, and a bulk book order form can be found starting on p. 167.)

Reflection: What were the five most important things that you learned from this book?

1.

2.

3.

4.

5.

Here's a great life rule for a strong person (a life rule is a rule that you try to apply at all times): "Respect Always!"

When you respect always, it means that you respect:

- your job by giving your best effort

- others through your words and actions

- yourself by taking care of yourself and by trying to make a good choice in every situation

Do you see what word the underlined letters above spell out? That's right, using this life rule will make it more likely that you'll have a good life filled with _joy_!

EPILOGUE

A cultural revolution is needed

In my opinion, we need a cultural revolution in order to successfully address our "Respect Crisis." We are way beyond only needing to put Band-Aids® on symptoms instead addressing the real problem. Dramatic action needs to be taken to significantly increase the low level of respect in our society in order to reduce the devasting symptoms of the problem (bullying, school and work underachievement, the onset of health problems at an early age, broken families, violence, crime, etc.). Here are some suggestions for how we can work together to make this cultural revolution happen:

- Help people learn the five tools that they need in order to build a good life and then encourage people to use these tools to build a good life (that's what this book was written to do)

- Tell your friends and family about the book. Mention to them that they can read a free excerpt at respectclub.org

- If you feel that the book is worthy, please consider writing an online review or leaving a rating at your favorite bookseller website

- Encourage parents you know to read the book with the hope that it will help them model, teach, encourage, and recognize respect

- Ask students to submit a comment on a regular basis about how they had respect for their job, others, and/or themselves to the Respect Club blog which can be accessed through the respectclub.org website. (All submissions are approved before they're published on the blog.) Encourage students to take a few minutes to view this blog a couple of times a week. This may help motivate and encourage them to practice being strong.

- Suggest to your school administration that they allow elementary school teachers as well as middle school ELA teachers to read the book aloud to their classes during read aloud time. (We provide books at our cost to teachers who are willing to do this. Please see p. 171.)

- Consider forming a group of parents, possibly along with a group of students, to meet with your school administrators, school board members, teachers, community leaders, business leaders, and politicians about starting a Respect Club™ to help model, teach, encourage, and recognize respect in your schools and throughout your community. A Respect Club taps into the awesome power of everyone working together toward the common goal of creating a community filled with respect. (Please go to respectclub.org for detailed information.)

Respect for your job
Respect for others
+   Respect for yourself
A good life

"If you know that it's a bad (disrespectful) choice - JUST DON'T DO IT." ™

"No one can make you feel inferior without your consent."
- Eleanor Roosevelt

INDEX OF TRUE STORIES BY TOPIC
(**bold** page numbers are for stories written for ages 15 and up)

Respect Club

Please check out respectclub.org for information about how to start a Respect Club in your school or in your school district. The mission of Respect Club is to help schools, communities, and parents' model, teach, encourage, and recognize respect.

Respect Club T-shirts, etc.

Please visit respectclub.org for more information about our trademarked T-shirts and other merchandise.

The ABC's of Behavior™ (info from respectclub.org)

Strong - when a person chooses to make a good choice just because it's a good choice and they don't really care about what disrespectful people say, do, or think about their choice (They make the good choice of having good character, displaying a positive attitude, fulfilling their responsibilities, giving their best effort, and demonstrating self-control.)

Complying - when a person chooses to make a good choice, but only to avoid punishment or to get a reward

Bad Choice - when a person chooses to make a bad choice even though they know it's a bad choice (often they're being selfish by doing what they feel like doing instead of what they know is a good choice)

Aggression - when a person tries to hurt others with their words or their body. This is the lowest level of behavior.

A Strong Person C.A.R.E.S.™ (info from respectclub.org)

Character, Attitude, Responsibility, Effort, and Self-control

Recommended books

True Love Lasts **by James Wegert**

Written by a school counselor who partially messed up his life by making bad dating choices, *True Love Lasts* communicates vital wholesome down-to-earth information to teens and young adults about what to look for in a person to date, how to date, and how to make a good marriage decision - with the goal of helping more people to have lifelong loving marriages.

The Money Book for the Young, Fabulous & Broke **by Suze Orman**

This book, for teens and up, will help you to develop the crucial skill of being able to control your spending by living on a budget.

Getting Real: Helping Teens Find Their Future **- by Kenneth Gray**

This book, along with the website bls.gov, can help teens to start the process of selecting a career with good job opportunities - a career that you'll enjoy and that will allow you to support yourself and possibility one day a family.

Request for comments, suggestions, etc.

Please feel free to let us know what you didn't agree with in this book. Do you have a suggestion for improving the book (topics for additional chapters, more information needed in a particular chapter, etc.) - we would like to know! Please send us an email at sbookpublishing@gmail.com. Your input may be used to improve future editions of the book. (Please don't include any last names in your email. Your email address will not be shared with anyone for any reason.)

BULK BOOK ORDER FORM

Save by ordering direct from the publisher

"How to become a strong person and build a good life" books:

10-49 copies - $7.50* per copy with free shipping
50-999 copies - $6.50* per copy with free shipping
(Please request a quote for quantities of 1000 or more.)

$4.50* per copy with free shipping for teachers who are willing to read parts of the book aloud to their students during read-aloud time. (Free if you already bought the book through TPT.)

\# of books requested_____   Cost_____

PA residents add 6% tax or include
a copy of your tax-exempt form   _____

                                        Total _____

Please send your name, email address, shipping address, and check/money order (made payable to Strong Book Publishing) and mail it to:

Strong Book Publishing
PO Box 5234
Lancaster, PA 17606-5234

(We will send you a confirmation email for the order. Your information is never shared for any reason.) Individual books are also available through your favorite online bookseller.

* Please note that prices are subject to change without notice. Please allow up to 3 weeks for delivery. If you have any questions, please email us at sbookpublishing@gmail.com. Thank you!

ABOUT THE AUTHOR

James Wegert has three college degrees and is certified as an elementary and secondary school counselor (for 91 more years or until he kicks the bucket - whichever comes first), but he's learned the most from the School of Hard Knocks (making bad choices). Based upon his education and experience, he feels that the level of respect in our society is way too low - and that this low level of respect is a crisis that's causing all types of problems in our society. He wrote this book and started Respect Club (respectclub.org) to help address this crisis. He's a big baseball fan, hence the baseball acronyms - designed to help you remember the parts of each tool, at the beginning of some chapters. He's periodically available to give informative and somewhat humorous "How to become a strong person and build a good life" presentations based upon the book to schools, colleges, and to communities within commuting distance of Lancaster, PA. The presentation is also available electronically, with your school and the names of some of your school personnel magically mentioned during the presentation, to schools located more than an hour away from Lancaster, PA. The author can be contacted by sending an email to questions@respectclub.org.

"Any dream worth going after is worth the work that it's going to take to achieve it!" ™

"Every day is an opportunity to be strong - please make the most of it and have a good life!"

Respect Always! - no excuses™

Best Wishes!
- Mr. W.

Made in the USA
Middletown, DE
27 June 2023

33882057R00109